[silent alarm]

"We all have two selves: the task-oriented self that's used to getting jobs done, and a thoughtful, reflective self. Which of these selves wakes up first in the morning? For all too many of us, it's our task-oriented self. The alarm goes off (what an awful name—why isn't it the opportunity clock or the it's-going-to-be-a-great-day clock?). We leap out of bed and jump into our task-oriented self. We eat while we're trying to wash, we jump into our car and get right on the car phone. We run from this meeting to that meeting, including lunch and dinner, and then finally get back home after nine and fall into bed exhausted, not even having any energy to say 'good-night' to anyone who might be lying next to us.

The next day the alarm goes off and we're at it again. Pretty soon we're caught up in a rat race. The problem with a rat race is, even if you win, you're still a rat. If you want to get out of the rat race, read John Blumberg's *Silent Alarm*. It might change your life."

       —Ken Blanchard, co-author of *The One Minute Manager*® and *Leading at a Higher Level*

"In our rush-rush world, it's easy to forget who and what matter most. *Silent Alarm* is a much needed catalyst to remind us to slow down and savor every blessing that graces our personal and professional life. Read it and reap!"

       —Sam Horn, Author of *Tongue Fu!*® and *POP! Stand Out in Any Crowd*, and 14-time emcee of the Maui Writers Conference

"Hope fuses into one's life through often curious pathways—including adversity as a springboard of such hope. *Silent Alarm* is written to be a beacon of fresh hope in a time of swirling confusion and disappointment. The truth of each page can be a fresh springboard of silent hope for the reader. It is a book to be well worn!"
> —Bob Danzig, former CEO of Hearst Newspapers, author, and speaker

"*Silent Alarm* is a page-turner with profound messages applicable to leaders who struggle with busyness conflicting with eternal opportunities. We, as leaders, have an opportunity to make a difference in the lives of others. This book is a vivid reminder of that responsibility."
> —Joy Flora, President of Merry Maids

"*Silent Alarm* is a most inspiring book to which I shall return again and again in my encouragement of living on purpose. I don't think a wiser wake-up call exists."
> —Richard Leider, author of the bestsellers
> *Repacking Your Bags* and *The Power of Purpose*

"This refreshing story disarms the façade of what you do to reveal the essence of who you are. In today's high-pressure, fast-paced business environment, *Silent Alarm* delivers a sabbatical that beckons the soul of every business professional. Taken to heart, this book has the potential to transform both your own personal journey as well as the organization in which you live it."
> —Richard Green, Retired President
> and COO of Blistex

"I loved this book! In its simplicity, it has had a profound impact on my life as I'm sure it will on yours. We are all so caught up in 'busyness' that we spend most of our lives skimming the surface—until a tragedy forces us to look within our hearts and souls to find what is truly important. John's beautiful spirit, compassion, and love for people permeate this powerful story, and we all will be better because of it. Thank you, John, for disarming our snooze buttons!"

—Barbara Glanz, author of *Handle with CARE* and *CARE Packages for the Workplace*

"*Silent Alarm* is a rich story with heart and punch. It is easy to live life with more speed than direction. This book helps the reader find direction through the eyes of Jack, a man addicted to success but lacking in direction. Jack discovers twelve values for his life, but only after he is forced to slow down and ask the right questions."

—Jim Goetz, Senior VP and Chief Information Officer of The ServiceMaster Company

"Here's your wake-up call! As a masterful storyteller, John has provided us with a way to get reconnected to what really matters and create a turning point in our lives and work."

—Mark LeBlanc, author of *Growing Your Business!* 2007-2008 President, National Speakers' Association

a parable of hope for busy professionals

[silent alarm]

John G. Blumberg

Rosedale Press

Copyright ©2005 John G. Blumberg

ISBN: 0-9765266-1-1

Library of Congress Control Number: 2005931067

Submit all requests for reprinting to:
Greenleaf Book Group LP
4425 Mopac South, Suite 600
Longhorn Bldg., 3rd Floor
Austin, TX 78735
(512) 891-6100

Published in the United States by Rosedale Press

Composition by Greenleaf Book Group
Cover Design by Greenleaf Book Group

First Edition
10 9 8 7 6 5 4 3

*This book is dedicated
to my wife Cindy
and our three children
Ryan, Kelly, and Julie.*

*You give me reason
to stay awake.*

Acknowledgments

In 1996, when I left behind an eighteen-year career I loved to begin my journey in professional speaking, a dear friend, Brad Preber, booked me for my first paid speaking engagement. The evening following that speaking engagement, Brad handed me a wrapped gift. Inside were a pipe and a silk robe. I must have looked a bit puzzled. He smiled and said, "I know you are going to be a great speaker, but I am convinced you are going to be a wonderful author as well. I thought these might come in handy as you write." I didn't wear the robe or smoke the pipe, but I haven't forgotten about them or Brad's genuine encouragement.

Brad was the first of many who inspired me beyond what I thought I was capable of doing. Kevin Freiberg was my first mentor in the speaking industry. He is both a friend and a hero in my eyes, and will be forever. My mastermind group—Barbara Glanz, Manny Garza, and Joe Healey—challenged and encouraged me to look past what seemed impossible. And this book may never have developed if it hadn't been for that late April afternoon when my long-term business coach, Mark LeBlanc, said, "John, the time to begin your book has definitely arrived. You have a unique message to share and the time has come for you to share it."

Maybe my deepest thanks goes to my "pilot readers," those brave souls who were willing to read the very first version of the manuscript. I picked a wide variety of people. The only thing they had in common was that they loved me enough to tell me the truth and I loved them enough to accept their genuine feedback: Mac Anderson, Greg Asimakoupoulos, Ken Bansemer, Carol Beu, Steve

Blumberg, Martha Brophy, Jim Brown, Suzanne Burnett, Forrest Cottrell, Natalie Couvillon, Rich Curran, Kevin Freiberg, Manny Garza, Russ Gates, Barbara Glanz, Sister Madelyn Gould, Shawn Harter, Mary Jo Hazard, Steve Hazard, Dave Houser, Bonnie Hudson, Michael and Maria Kazlauskas, Mark LeBlanc, Jim Lemon, Patrick McWard, Ryan O'Neill, Diane Overgard, Janice Rubin, BK Simerson, Bob Thames, Jerry Tomas, and Ron Willingham. This book would never have seen the light of day without your honesty and encouragement.

I remember other authors telling me that writing a book is easy but the editing process will kill you. Editing was a tedious part of the process, but each of my three editors—John Atkinson, Hilary Turner, and Jay Hodges—truly became my partners and helped make this project enjoyable. They put their hearts and souls into *Silent Alarm*. I felt blessed to have them in such a critical role. The entire team at the Greenleaf Book Group has been awesome. I couldn't imagine a team more creative, kind, or professional.

Then there are the people who were encouraging every step of the way. Dave Ferguson, Al Gustafson, Dave Sparkman, Roycee Kerr, and so many others have given me strength for the journey. And, of course, everyone should be blessed with a mom who becomes their biggest fan. Etna Blumberg has always cheered me on!

The book you hold in your hands is the result of each of these people. Their signatures are on this story. Their genuine input made it come to life in a way I never thought possible.

I will be forever grateful to each of you.

John Blumberg
Naperville, Illinois
April 5, 2005

Something happened in the aftermath of September 11, 2001. People around the globe, and certainly in the United States, became more reflective. We began to rethink our priorities and recommit ourselves to the individuals we love and the things we deem important. Many garnered the courage to say, "I'm not going to sell out my family anymore just to keep up or get ahead at work. I'm going to check in, reengage and 'be there' for the people I care about most." Yet old habits die hard. Ask the average person, "How much has really changed in your life as a result of 9/11?" and the answer, unfortunately, for many is, "Not much." It is as though we received a wake-up call and, to use John Blumberg's words, "rolled over and hit the snooze button."

What's the matter with us? Our standard of living has never been higher, but our quality of life is at an all-time low. We have more technological firepower with which to stay connected, yet we feel more disengaged than ever. We were told that technology would make us more efficient and give us more time. The reality is that we've taken that time and filled it with more work. We are drawn to television and print ads that prey on our insecurities and low self-esteem. They tell us that if we drive the right car, don a certain watch, wear the right clothes, and so on, we can be somebody—sexier, wealthier, healthier, and more powerful. Needless to say, we've become addicted to stuff. Is it any wonder that our consumer debt is off the Richter scale? We are trapped in unfulfilling jobs because we are overextended. We buy things we don't need with money we don't have to impress people we don't even like. We've come to a place of needing what we want instead of wanting what we need. We live in a society where there is a growing propensity to love things and use people instead of loving people and using things. Blumberg will tell you, "Our dream is at risk."

Maybe it's just easier to go through the motions than to pay attention to the messages life sends us. Maybe it's easier to live our hurried, busy, boring, and often routine lives than it is to slow down and ask the tough questions that lead to a truly meaningful life. The book that you are holding in your hand is not likely to let you off the hook—it will encourage you to stop being a victim and to see that the way you live your life is your choice. *Silent Alarm* challenges you to avoid the snooze buttons, resist the temptation to just get back to normal, and slow down long enough to consider what really matters.

What I love about John Blumberg is that he inspires me to think about life at a deeper level. Perhaps that is because he has been blessed with an uncanny ability to find the lessons in life that many of us are oblivious to. Of course, you can't find what you are not looking for. Many people are reticent to dig deeply because they are afraid of what they might find. So, they resolve to live on the surface, where it is safe—and superficial. John is fearless; he looks more diligently and digs more deeply than most. The good news is that you and I are the beneficiaries of his courageous quest. Provocative, thoughtful, and loaded with incredible insight, Blumberg delivers a captivating story that will enrich your life and improve your business.

When John asked me to read the original manuscript I agreed, because John is a friend. As I started to pore through *Silent Alarm*, I soon lost sight of the fact that it was a friend's manuscript. The story quickly engaged me and, like Jack, whom you will soon meet, I found myself eagerly awaiting the next lesson on the pages to come. My focus intently shifted to some tough questions that caused me to pause, reflect, and consider the road I'm on. And that's a good thing, because with three active kids, a wife I cherish and enjoy, and a job that takes me all over the world, I'm usually going 90 miles per hour with my hair on fire. It always seems like pulling over to the side of the road just to stop and think is for those who have way too much time on their hands. My bad.

Silent Alarm unloads, with both barrels, a message we would all do well to embrace: If you don't make time to reflect, foolishness prevails, because you never figure out what you really want out of life and you end up just going through the motions. Before you know it, you've wasted more time than you care to admit wondering how you got this way or how the world you could've affected, but didn't, came to be. Are you living a meaningful life or are you on the treadmill just trying to keep up? Are you living life intentionally or accidentally? Are you willing to speak out against the things that outrage you? Are you willing to stand for the things you believe in? Are you willing to look in the mirror and ask, "If the world—my government, company, church, or community—is going to be a better place, what about me needs to change?" These are difficult, but important questions—the kind of questions you will be compelled to ask as you read *Silent Alarm*.

Warning! This a wake-up call to get you off the treadmill and help you stop living life so unconsciously. If you let this story take hold, it will challenge you to consider what *meaningful* success looks like in your life. In subtle and sometimes not-so-subtle ways, it will push, prod, cajole, and inspire you to stop letting the world call the shots by imposing its definition of success on you. The world will define success by telling you what you must have or do. *Silent Alarm* will tell you that success is much more about who you become in the process of accomplishing other things. I invite you to let this gripping story of courage, patience, and unconditional love inspire you to be who you were created to be, do what you are called to do, and live a life that is intentional.

After reading *Silent Alarm* I was reminded of the words of the great Danish philosopher, Søren Kierkegaard, who said, "All change is preceded by crisis." Whether it's religiously buckling up after a major accident, going on a strict, low-cholesterol diet after a heart attack, holding CEOs and boards more accountable for their decisions in the wake of corporate scandals, or clamping down on security after one of the most devastating terrorist attacks the world has ever seen, many of us can identify with Kierkegaard's message. Blumberg's question in *Silent Alarm*: will we wake up to the lessons life teaches before we find ourselves in a crisis of overwhelming proportion?

Many authors offer interesting but shallow ideas that numb us with Band-Aid solutions. Not John Blumberg; he is the real deal. He doesn't have a superficial bone in his body. His genuine and sincere nature is uniquely interwoven with his bold plunge beneath the surface and into the depths of discovering the real issues among us. Taken to heart, this book offers much more than a quick fix. *Silent Alarm* will give you more freedom, cause you to love more deeply and define your dream more meaningfully. But only if you have the guts to act upon what you learn. In the end, the pearls of wisdom that jump off the following pages will help you become more alive.

Silent Alarm is a must-read that hits you at a visceral level and inspires you to pass it on. It not only celebrates truth, it celebrates the greatness within all of us. Never have leaders and professionals in our business community been more in need of the message this story conveys. The issues we face in our business community are complex and significant. They will not be fixed by a nation or even by a corporation. That's because individuals, not organizations, create problems. The real cure will only take hold in the values, purpose, motives, and hearts of people like you and me. We can wait for the next person to lead, or we can choose to wake up with courage to the purpose we have been called to live.

Your personal alarm is ringing. Can you hear it? Read on.

Kevin Freiberg
Author of *Nuts!: Southwest Airlines' Crazy Recipe for Business and Personal Success* and *Guts!: Companies that Blow the Doors off Business-as-Usual*
San Diego, California
February 3, 2005

Chapter 1

Jack hadn't heard Susan hit the snooze button three times that morning. He'd been working round the clock on yet another crisis at work. All the days seemed to run together. Even years had become a blur. He didn't even realize it was Sunday morning. It didn't matter. He just knew he was late getting to the office. Very late. Half asleep, he blew off shaving, quickly showered, dried off, pulled on his nearest clean clothes, gave Susan a quick kiss, and flew out the door. He took no more than eight minutes from bed to street.

It crossed his mind, as he drove down the dark, cold, and empty road that the concept of "running late" to the office on a Sunday morning was quite ridiculous. But then ridiculous somehow seemed normal. Normal was relative . . . and this was normal. Nonetheless, he was focused on beating the 6:08 a.m. daily freight train to the Southern Road crossing.

This morning would be close. He eyed the long train far off in the distance. There was plenty of time. He was an expert at calculating safe passage . . . and with three children, a beautiful wife, a lovely home and a successful career, he wasn't about to take any chances. Jack simply wasn't a risk-taker. And with his eyes focused on the train in the distance to his left, it simply wasn't a risk.

The twenty-ton explosion of steel came from the right.

Chapter 2

Susan hurried past the nursing station in the center of the intensive care unit. She'd been told that Jack was in room 573, the last door on the right.

She stiffened at the eerie silence as she hesitated just inside the room. Jack lay motionless in a tangle of tubes and surgical dressings. The tubes ran like cobwebs across his body. Clicking and beeping machines whispered almost inaudibly in the background.

She barely noticed Dr. Berry enter the room. He glanced toward Jack, then looked her in the eye and said, "It's too early to tell."

She bit her lip as her eyes filled with tears.

After sobbing alone in the washroom, Susan finally sank onto a couch in the waiting area. She hunkered down, waiting for permission to see Jack again.

The voice of her father Carl drifted over to her from the elevator bank. Three weeks had passed since their last conversation because of busy schedules and various distractions, but she knew his voice in a heartbeat.

When Susan saw her father, her body shook with sobs. He felt the depth of her despair and tried to comfort her. His embrace was as reassuring as the blanket she had clung to so often in childhood.

Susan sat with her daddy. The TV news blaring in the background seemed so irrelevant. It would be five agonizing hours before they heard anything more about Jack's condition.

Faded memories danced in her weary mind. Images of innocence . . . of simplicity. Life had become so busy and so complicated.

Considering the mounting tragedies in the world, life these past few years had remained pretty normal for her, Jack, and the kids—although 1999 felt like a century away. Throughout the nineties it had seemed that everything was going right. Both she and Jack had been building successful careers. Oh sure, life had been busy. Yet with the conveniences of outstanding day-care centers for the kids, maids for the house, and dry cleaning delivered directly to the front door, they were able to manage. Their lifestyle was affordable because of their dual incomes, incredible profit sharing, lucrative stock options, and escalating mutual funds. The purchase of their dream home four years ago had been a promising beginning to a new chapter in their storybook-perfect life.

The year after the move, Susan thought long and hard about the financial impact of becoming a stay-at-home mom.

After twelve more months of earning a substantial salary, she finally decided to try it out. She worried about getting bored and falling behind in a rapidly changing world, but it seemed like the right thing to do. After all, Jack was still the golden boy at the office. His recent promotion had made the economic decision even easier. It seemed nothing could go wrong. This was Susan's version of a normal life, and it appeared to be pretty close to perfect. But clouds began to gather when the longest economic buildup in U.S. history began to fall apart.

Jack started receiving new e-mails almost every week from former Harvard MBA classmates who had just been rightsized into unemployment. It hit particularly close to home when Mike called. Mike had been the best man in Jack and Susan's wedding. Annual Christmas letters had kept them up to speed with the basics about each other's lives, but Jack hadn't talked to him in two years. It was the longest they'd gone without speaking since becoming best friends freshman year of high school. But Jack and Mike had one of those life-long friendships: years could pass without a word, yet the moment they reconnected, the distance of time collapsed.

When the call came, Jack had been thrilled to hear from Mike, although the ringing of the phone had awoken him from a deep sleep. For thirty minutes they laughed about the good old days before moving on to more recent events. Jack noticed a significant switch in Mike's tone as he shared the news of his layoff, which had come as a total surprise because Mike had been promoted two months prior. But Wall Street was king and the company's stock performance had fallen short of analysts' expectations. Jack had sensed how Mike felt: vulnerable, helpless, and deeply disappointed.

Mike's expectations of continued corporate success had prompted him and his wife Cheryl to upgrade to a nicer home just months earlier. Jack offered his condolences, assured his friend that everything would be fine, and pledged to keep his ears open for opportunities.

Jack thought about that call for a good week and something bothered him. Three times the next week as he was driving home from work, Jack had called Mike just to chat. The third call would mark the last conversation they would have for quite a while. With Wall Street expectations driving aggressive performance measures, Jack couldn't be distracted for long and was again quickly focused on work. Everything seemed back to normal.

* * *

As Susan sat in the waiting room, she asked her dad if he would call Mike. He smiled and said Mike was already driving up from Memphis. She sighed in relief.

Tears began to run down Susan's cheeks as she pictured Jack at 1 a.m. on Christmas morning putting the final touches on the kids' gifts. He wasn't a technology wizard, but he had no trouble setting up the new computer system for the children. She remembered sharing a companionable nightcap with him before they retired to bed that night.

Susan opened her eyes to see the lead surgeon standing over her. He was not smiling. She grabbed her dad's hand.

Chapter 3

Jack was in critical but stable condition. Dr. Berry quietly explained that the swelling in Jack's brain had been relieved and it appeared for the moment that he would live. Walking again, however, was almost out of the question. Susan's dad tightened his grip on her hand as he tried to bolster her courage.

Dr. Berry went on to say the next forty-eight hours would be critical. It appeared that due to the damage to his spine, Jack would likely be paralyzed from the waist down. It was unclear at this point if the damage to the brain had destroyed Jack's chances of ever speaking again. This was too much for Susan. She collapsed against her father.

About an hour later, the head nurse arrived to escort Susan back to Jack's room. She reminded Susan that she could only stay a few minutes. The room seemed inviting: the pale yellow walls cheered up an otherwise sterile environment.

She walked slowly toward Jack. It seemed like he was only sleeping, but the tubes reminded Susan of the seriousness of his condition. She walked around to the far side of the bed and moved close, gently placing her hand on his knee. Then she closed her eyes and began to pray.

Finally she whispered, "Jack, I love you." She didn't expect a response. It didn't matter. It was enough to be with him. Even with the two deep cuts across his right cheek, he looked perfect to her. She closed her eyes and softly gripped his limp right hand.

Her mind wandered to the day they'd first met. It was a warm, sunny afternoon on the campus of the University of Tennessee. They were both in the spring semester of their sophomore years. She was on the verge of starting the core courses of her journalism major and he was headed into the challenging curriculum of a finance degree. If it hadn't been for an English class, their paths might never have crossed. And if she hadn't dropped her book . . . and he hadn't picked it up, their relationship might never have blossomed.

Susan closed her eyes again and enjoyed this moment of peace in the middle of the storm. Suddenly the large gray machine to the left started screeching. Her heart was still jumping as three nurses hurried through the door. Two ran for Jack while the other grabbed Susan and rushed her out. Standing in the hallway, Susan didn't know if she'd just seen Jack breathe his last breath.

It had been a long night. The sudden scare had turned out to be more about the machine than about Jack. Yet everyone was reminded of how uncertain the future was. Jack remained in critical, but increasingly stable condition. Susan and Carl had finally fallen asleep on chairs in the waiting area.

The sun was not yet up on this wintry Monday morning when Susan's mother Jeanne called. The kids were up and getting ready for school. Chip, their oldest, didn't want to leave without talking to his mom. Susan reached inside for the courage to be strong. In a soft voice she told Chip not to worry, to work hard at school, and to help Grandma with anything she needed. She also told him she would be home as soon as she could.

Athletic and well built, Chip was a younger version of Jack. Jack was so proud of Chip's roles as quarterback and captain of the freshman football team. Though competitive,

Chip had a strong character and a soft heart. His parents were his heroes.

Susan managed a few more words, telling him to give hugs to his younger brother and sister. He would have done that anyway, but she enjoyed reminding him. She was on her last three words, "I love you," when her voice cracked. It was then that Chip realized that things were going to be totally different from then on.

As Susan handed the cell phone back to her dad, Mike arrived.

He brought Susan a special sense of comfort. He was almost a part of Jack. The two were twin sons of different mothers. Although their college days took them on separate paths, they couldn't wait for fall, winter, and spring breaks to reconnect. Time, miles, and a few children had made their routine connections fewer and further between. However, at this moment in the waiting room, the true substance of their friendship was clearly evident.

Susan suggested that Mike take the next scheduled visit with Jack. Mike was moved by her generous offer. Shortly before 8:30 a.m. he followed the nurse to room 573. As Mike walked in, he felt weak at the sight of Jack, but he was filled with gratitude to have this time with him. It was one of the healing moments that melts the façade of the everyday and makes life meaningful.

He walked over and looked at Jack's silent and motionless state. Like Susan, Mike felt the need to softly speak to him. No response was needed. Mike felt a lump gather in his throat. It hurt to vocalize his thoughts, but he spoke anyway.

And the more he spoke, the more easily the words flowed. He spoke of simple things, because he knew that was all that mattered.

Mike knew his time with Jack was running short. He pulled three wallet-sized pictures from his pocket. He'd grabbed them from his refrigerator on the way out the door. The photos had been included in Jack and Susan's last Christmas card, and Mike still couldn't believe how much Chip's freshman picture resembled the Jack he had met on the first day of high school.

Mike found a roll of white adhesive tape on the sink and tore off a small piece. He taped Chip's picture to the raised bed rail on Jack's right side. Then he tore off two more pieces to hang Bobby and Katie's pictures to the right of Chip. He knew that eventually his friend's eyes would open, and when they did, there couldn't be a more welcome sight than the three photographs.

Mike heard the nurse coming in the door and realized his twenty minutes had passed. He patted the top of Jack's right hand.

Mike was exhausted from driving all night. After a long visit with Susan and Carl in the waiting room, he departed for the nearby motel, promising to return later that afternoon.

Chapter 5

Jack's parents had passed away many years ago. Jack shared a shallow but friendly relationship with Carl. They enjoyed each other's company, but living a couple hundred miles apart, they did not get together often. They didn't have a lot in common, other than Susan.

Carl had been quite successful in business, but few realized this. He had no desire to boast because he felt it really had little to do with what was important in life. Few of his heroes were great business successes.

The business world was simply a context in which he lived out his life. Susan grew up with a very clear understanding of her dad's priorities. She knew what he really valued.

In the past few years, Carl had recommitted himself to his original values, and he continued to believe that good could come from all difficult situations.

While he was trying to provide comfort to his daughter in the waiting room, she raised her hand to stop him. In theory, she believed his words, but she wondered how much suffering one person needed.

Carl nodded in understanding. A number of terrible events had happened in the early years of this new millennium, and any one of those events would have been more than enough.

Susan had been thankful that her family had not been directly affected. But Carl knew it was the subtle impact that could kill you. He wondered if anyone would wake up to the message and find good in the bad. He had begun to lose hope. He wondered if mankind had changed . . . or if we had always been this way.

Carl reminded Susan of their first visit to Disneyland. She had begged her daddy to take her. Susan was so excited when her parents and her brother, Steve, piled into the car for the long drive to Anaheim, California.

Retelling this story, Carl quickly captured Susan's attention and the little energy she had left. They laughed as they remembered the magic of the visit. Susan commented on how there was nothing funny about Space Mountain. Carl agreed with her: it took a really sick person to put a roller coaster in the dark. Yet he also remembered how he had begged her to go with him on that ride.

Sitting in the bleak hospital waiting area, Carl told Susan that life was much like Space Mountain.

"Life is like a roller coaster in the dark," he explained. "The open-air coasters let you see your way. They may look scary, but you know the what, when, and how of the experience. Space Mountain is different. You never know what is going to happen next. Will you be going up, down, down again, left, or right? You don't know, so you just have to sit back and live through the experience."

Susan could see the similarities. But she was taken back by what her father said next.

He looked at Susan and said, "You know what's most amazing? Each individual experience is usually determined before passengers even get on the ride. Think about how the same exact set of metal tracks provoke so many unique emotions: amusement, fear, boredom."

Susan couldn't help but remember what was going through her mind as she stood in line for Space Mountain that day. Looking up at her daddy, she had simply decided to trust him.

Monday had been a long day of waiting. Susan had finally had a chance to talk with Bobby and Katie when they arrived home from school. All of the kids had been excited to see Grandpa when he woke up just before dinner from his nap. Susan had encouraged him in the afternoon to return to her house to get some rest. Because the kids were in good hands with their grandparents, Susan stayed put. She felt a sense of emptiness when her dad left the hospital, but also recognized a need to be alone to collect her thoughts.

Mike had returned briefly that afternoon, took another of the scheduled visits with Jack, and then returned to his motel to catch up on some work. Ordinarily he would have stayed at the hospital, but he didn't want to do anything that might jeopardize his new job.

Jack was still in critical condition, but he continued to stabilize. This news gave Susan some needed hope and energy, which, for a while, offset the fact that she really hadn't slept much. Carl returned, quite refreshed, just before the ten o'clock news. He kept watch as Susan dozed on the uncomfortable couch.

Just after midnight, Monica, the head nurse on the night shift, stopped by to introduce herself. She had been off for the weekend and was making rounds to catch up on the patients who had arrived since her last shift.

A true nursing veteran, Monica had been on this floor working the same shift for over twenty-five years. She loved her job. More accurately, she came to love each patient. She had struggled with the challenges placed on health-care workers by managed care, but somehow never let it get in the way of her relationship with her patients and their families. She enjoyed being a nurse, but would have somehow expressed her love for others, no matter what her occupation. This role, however, was especially suited for her. While others complained, especially on the night shift, she simply found opportunity.

Monica provided incredible care to her patients. She took the time to get to know each one of them. Although she was thrilled to see patients recover, she was always a little sad to say good-bye to them.

Each year she sent more than three hundred holiday cards to former patients. It was her greatest source of joy during the holiday season. Each card was personalized and written with the same care the patient had come to know during their stay on her floor.

Monica took better care of her patients than she did of herself. Her shoes were scuffed and worn; in fact, she considered her current pair to be relatively new even after five years.

She always wore her white uniform. She just never could adapt to the trend of more casual styles, although she certainly had no problem with the other nurses who had. A plump, rosy woman, Monica certainly enjoyed her food. She had no desire to be like the women in fashion magazines. Jogging was out of the question, but then again, so was smoking. She was a balanced piece of work.

Monica loved laughing as much as she loved delicious foods. She was constantly joking with her patients and their visitors. Deep down she was an introvert, but you would never know it: she was never at a loss for words when she was working.

Although Monica had been engaged once, she had never married. She was quite content lavishing affection on her patients and her little nieces and nephews. "Aunt Monica" was their favorite, a second mom. She spent most of her weekends attending their extracurricular activities. It helped that her whole family lived within a ten-mile radius.

She had already read the patients' histories before she walked into the waiting room and she knew everything that had transpired since Jack had arrived on Sunday morning. She had already been in to meet Jack, although Jack was not aware of her presence, and she'd immediately noticed the pictures of Chip, Bobby, and Katie attached to the bed rail. She smiled at the gift that had been bestowed upon this new patient. She knew that medical problems would be only the beginning of Jack's road to recovery, and she looked forward to her nightly role in his journey. She felt sure she had just met someone she was going to really like.

Carl was surprised to hear Monica call him by name. Monica spoke with him for a few minutes and quickly filled in the mental blanks of Jack's family situation. She had a memory that lasted forever, and this conversation would come in handy as she tried to care for her newest patient.

Susan was still in a deep sleep. She, like Jack, was still oblivious to Monica's presence. Both of them were in for a wonderful surprise.

Carl enjoyed their conversation. Since the discussion had focused only on Jack, Susan, and their family, he didn't find out much about Monica. But he quickly realized he'd just met someone very special. What he didn't know was just how special she was.

Chapter 7

S usan slept quite well, only to awaken just after three o'clock when Mike arrived. He'd awoken in the middle of the night, and was unable to fall asleep again, so he returned to the waiting room.

Carl had taken the last two visits to see Jack. On the second visit, Jack had actually moved his right arm and squeezed Carl's hand as he stood by his bedside. Monica happened to walk in the room at that moment. They both smiled as they realized Jack had taken a big step forward on his journey.

Mike rejected Susan's insistence for him to take the 4:00 a.m. visit. He knew it was more important that she get in to see Jack. Susan had been very touched by Mike's thoughtfulness in not only bringing them, but also hanging the kids' pictures on Jack's bedrail. She wished that her mind could slow down enough to think of doing such meaningful little things.

Susan was sitting in Jack's room when Monica made one of her rounds. Carl had mentioned the wonderful head nurse and it only took a moment in Monica's presence to confirm all that Susan had been told.

Soon Monica and Susan were chatting like lifelong friends. Monica asked about the children and Susan enjoyed giving a description of each of them. It felt good to share a bit about the kids because she hadn't been able to be with them in the last forty-eight hours.

Susan told Monica how Bobby and Katie did not follow in Chip's athletic footsteps. Bobby loved music, and had started learning to play drums at the age of four. Katie was the artist. Jack had framed one of her works for his office. Everyone commented on it and was shocked to hear it was his very young daughter's work.

Monica enjoyed learning about each of the children and drank in every word. She was sad about Jack's accident, but excited that this wonderful new family had entered her life.

Jack's vital signs continued to improve. Monica, however, had been in nursing long enough to know the uncertainty of the path that was ahead. Regardless, she and Susan were both encouraged.

Monica had to get moving on her rounds, but she knew this wouldn't be the last of her conversations with Susan— and she was looking forward to her first conversation with Jack. She just didn't know how soon that would be.

Chapter 8

Chip woke up early that Tuesday morning. He was excited to see the snow falling and was waiting to hear if school would be canceled. Snow days in Chicago were rare, but he was hoping that the combination of subzero temperatures and eight inches of snow might convince someone that it just wasn't worth it.

He put on his coat and fetched the morning newspaper for his grandma. Shivering from his quick run to and from the end of the long driveway, he looked at the front page and saw a picture of his dad's wrecked car in vivid color. All the blood drained from his face.

He knew things were serious, but as he looked at the picture he was amazed his dad was even alive. He wasn't the only one.

The media had jumped all over the accident to follow up on a series of stories they had done the previous autumn about inadequate signals at railroad crossings. They were now on a mission to prove their point. Reporters had called the house, but were surprised to find that Jeanne could be just as persistent as they were. Susan and her mother had been journalism majors so the tricks of the media were nothing new to them. The reporters would get their story one way or another, but it wouldn't come from Jack's family.

Chip was devastated as he read the story of the accident. He simply put his head down on the table and began to sob. Jeanne came and stood over him. She had conveniently tucked away the Monday paper before Chip had returned from school the previous day. She knew all she could do now was try to comfort him.

After a few minutes, Chip raised his head and demanded to go to the hospital. Jeanne made a vague promise and hoped for the best. Just minutes later the phone rang. It was Susan. She had great news. Jack had just opened his eyes for the first time since the accident. In the strange and wonderful way of the world, many eyes would be opened in the coming days.

S usan was filled with energy and infused Chip with a great sense of hope. She told him that Grandpa would pick him up after school and bring him to the hospital.

Monica had stayed on after her shift for a few minutes to celebrate Jack's next step on the road to recovery. She'd encouraged Susan to call home and suggested that she have Carl bring up Chip for a short visit after school. It was at times like this that Monica wished she could work twenty-four hours a day. She hated that she would not be there to meet Chip when he arrived.

She knew nurses on the afternoon shift were quite busy and she wasn't sure if Chip would get the personal welcome that she thought he needed. So she simply jotted him a quick note on some of her goofy stationery. She assured him that they would take great care of Jack, and that even while Chip slept at home, she would be wide awake helping his dad. She stuck the note with a little box of candy for him to share with Bobby and Katie. Monica didn't know when she would meet them, but hoped it would not be too long. She left the note and candy with Susan, who was amazed at her incredible thoughtfulness and wondered if she wrote such notes every day.

Monica stopped by the grocery on the way home. It was her Tuesday morning ritual. She was way too busy with family on the weekends to waste time doing such routine chores on Saturday and Sunday. Besides, it was senior citizens' morning at the grocery and she was thrilled to weave among them, calling many of them by name. She was in no hurry and would be in bed soon enough to get her required seven hours of sleep.

As soon as she got home, she put the ice cream in the freezer and a few other items in the refrigerator. Then she began to think about one of her greatest joys in life, a new tradition she'd started in the past year. She found herself wishing she could extend this tradition to one more patient.

Eighteen months had passed since her trip out West to Colorado Springs with her sister's family. She rarely took a two-week vacation and she had enjoyed every minute of it. They had all stayed at a dude ranch about ninety miles west of the city. It was her kind of excitement: simple and down to earth.

Monica wasn't a gambler. And she certainly didn't waste her money on the lottery. It was just by chance that they stopped at a run-down convenience store as they were driving out of Colorado Springs, headed towards the dude ranch. The only shiny thing in the store was the lottery ticket display and that caught everyone's eye. All the kids begged her to buy a lottery ticket. It took a lot of persuasion, but just before they left she gave in and bought one ticket.

The kids insisted on staying up late to watch the news for the on-the-air drawing. Monica wasn't very excited about being a vehicle to whet their appetite for gambling, but found it hard to contain her excitement when she realized she had won over $300.

Monica told everyone she'd use her winnings to treat them to a nice dinner on their last night in Colorado Springs.

The seven-day package at the dude ranch was awesome. She'd wanted the whole family to vacation at a dude ranch ever since she'd seen the movie *City Slickers*. Monica was game for almost everything. The opening-day horse ride and sunburn just about did her in, but she was not about to let anything stop her; she would always be a kid at heart.

Monica took no time at all adjusting to a daytime schedule, but still wasn't in any hurry to get to bed at night. Some of her favorite memories of the ranch involved singing by the campfire. Everyone had begged Aunt Monica to bring her guitar and she had been glad to comply.

Monica loved music and would have majored in it in college if it hadn't been for her passion to be a nurse. She couldn't read music, but she had an incredible ear and could quickly pick up almost any song. Her voice was beautiful, but she insisted that everyone sing with her. She especially enjoyed songs about the lessons of life.

She couldn't believe how fast the week of down-to-earth activities passed. They left the ranch just after the grand-finale luncheon to return to Colorado Springs for their last night. They checked into the hotel, showered, and headed up to Manitou Springs for their big dinner. Since they arrived with plenty of time to spare, they worked their way through the little gift shops. They had passed through several stores when they happened upon a shop called the Aspen Grove. It was small but filled to the brim with all the kinds of things Monica delighted in.

She and her niece Sarah browsed the shelves together. It was there that Sarah spotted the display of angels made of oxidizing copper. They were quite small and simple, but this only added to their rustic beauty. Each had a unique set of wings and stood about five or six inches tall. Every angel was slightly different from the others and each had its own name. They both fell in love with the first angel that Sarah picked up.

Monica was admiring the angel when Sarah suggested that she should buy a bunch of the figures to give to her patients. Sarah couldn't imagine a group more in need of a simple symbol of hope. Monica thought it was a brilliant idea, but told Sarah that it would cost quite a fortune.

Monica continued to admire the other angel designs. She was so absorbed in them she didn't notice that Sarah had disappeared until a few minutes later, when her niece returned.

Sarah smiled at her aunt and said, "I talked with everyone and told them about this angel. We all decided that after eating nonstop for the past seven days, the last thing we need is a big dinner. We want you to take your lottery winnings and buy as many angels as you can. Then you can take them back and give them to the patients who you think need them the most."

Monica loved the idea. She thanked her family for their thoughtfulness and told them she would be glad to give the angels on their behalf. And so she bought every rustic angel the shop had in stock. The final total, including the cost of shipping back to Chicago, came within three dollars of her winnings.

For the next year, Monica found much joy in sharing this small gift with the patients she thought needed it most. She always looked forward to presenting her little gift to each of these patients. It took a year, but her supply of angels finally ran out.

As she finished emptying the grocery bags, she couldn't get Jack and Susan out of her mind. More than ever, she wished she had just one more angel. The more she thought about it, the more she wanted to order one.

Then she remembered one of the figurines she had stashed in her closet because the box had been damaged in shipment from Colorado.

She pulled out a step stool and stretched to see if it was still where she had remembered putting it. It was still there, waiting for her. She pulled it down, dusted it off, and decided the box was not as damaged as she remembered. There was only a very slight dent in the side. She pulled out the white Styrofoam box inside and opened it to find the figure in perfect shape.

Monica decided this angel would do just fine. Little did she realize what a difference she was about to make.

The forecast caught Monica's attention. She never took any chances. She normally would get to bed by noon and set her alarm for 7:00 p.m. With the forecast of up to twenty-four inches, she wasn't going to take a chance. She would much rather be stuck at the hospital than stuck at home, so she set her alarm for 3:00 p.m. to check out the conditions.

There had been a break in the storm, but the forecast wasn't promising. A new front was approaching in the next four hours and record-breaking accumulations were predicted. Monica quickly showered, made herself a middle-of-the-night snack, grabbed the damaged gift box, and was out the door. It was freezing and already dark at four o'clock but traffic was light. No one on the staff was surprised to see Monica hours before her shift.

Carl and Chip had just returned to the waiting room from visiting Jack when Monica arrived. Chip had been anxious to see Jack and was relieved that things weren't quite as bad as he had expected after seeing the front-page story. He knew everything was still serious, but it was far better than what he had feared. They had not yet told him about what he couldn't see. He didn't expect his dad to speak or move his legs. But he wasn't aware that this condition might be permanent. When Jack opened his eyes for the second time, Chip was thrilled to be there. His tender age was no match for this situation. He didn't know what to say. Confused by the intensity of feelings and the rush of tears, he simply mumbled, "I love you, Dad."

This wasn't how Chip typically talked. He hadn't used these words in quite a while. With Jack's glazed look upon him, he repeated himself. Carl tried to hold back his tears, but didn't succeed. With one last look and a pat to his dad's right leg, Chip turned around and followed his grandpa back to the waiting room.

Susan and Mike were excited to hear Chip's news that Jack had opened his eyes again. They were discussing how grateful they were for Jack's improvement over the last forty-eight critical hours when Monica walked into the room. Susan was surprised to see their night-shift miracle arriving so early, and quickly turned to Chip to introduce her. Chip thanked her for the note and candy. Monica chatted with everyone for a moment. It felt like she was a long-lost member of the family. Then she turned to Chip and asked if he could come with her for a moment. Chip followed Monica to the nurses' station.

Monica reached for the worn little shopping bag from behind the counter and pulled out the slightly damaged angel box. She handed Chip the box and asked him to open it. Monica told him the story of the angels, and Chip was grateful that she had forgotten about the last damaged box. He carefully pulled out and opened the white Styrofoam container to reveal the little angel. Chip looked up and smiled. Monica asked him to follow her to room 573 to help her deliver the gift to Jack.

As they entered the room, Monica motioned for him to take the gift to his dad. Jack's eyes were closed. Chip didn't know if he was asleep or even if he could hear him, but he set the little angel on the crowded nightstand to Jack's right.

Chip gently sat down on the side of the bed. His eyes began to fill with tears. Monica stood by the door, watching and smiling.

Chip knew his dad couldn't see the angel, so he decided to describe her simple beauty to him. Monica was impressed by his elaborate description. She was touched as he continued bringing life to the little rustic angel through his words. And she was amazed these gentle words were coming from this athletic high school student sitting in front of her. Chip waited until the end of his narration to describe the angel's outstretched arms. Through Chip's words, the angel took on a beauty and dimension that Monica had never appreciated before.

As he finished speaking, Chip turned to Monica and told his dad that this angel had come from a wonderful nurse. He thought they were both angels of inspiration.

Just as Chip stood up, his dad opened his eyes and smiled for the first time.

Chip turned back to Monica, smiled and said, "Thank you."

Monica just stood there thinking that no gift goes only one direction. Her heart was filled with joy and humility.

For a moment, everyone in the room was as still as the little angel on the nightstand. Huge white flakes had begun to fall outside the window.

Susan noticed that Chip looked like a different person than the boy who had arrived just two hours before. Chip didn't have a chance to say a word before his grandpa threw him his coat and told him they'd better hurry before the snow began to accumulate. He gave his mom a hug and a kiss and went flying out the door with his grandpa.

The flakes were large, but gently falling. Two additional inches had fallen in the last thirty minutes and there seemed to be no end in sight.

Several accidents had already been reported, and Susan began to worry about Chip and Carl driving home. The last thing she needed was for something to happen to those two precious men in her life.

Susan was relieved when her cell phone rang and her mom announced that Chip and Carl were pulling into the driveway. The next thing she knew, Chip was on the phone. For the next five minutes, Chip told her the story of the angel. It was a shorter version than the one he had shared with

Grandpa on the way home. Susan smiled and was grateful once more for Monica's presence at the hospital.

Mike had taken the 6:00 p.m. visit, and then arranged a fast-food dinner to share with Susan in the waiting room. Then he returned to the motel, hoping to get a good night's sleep.

Susan had seen enough of the news and had heard the blizzard warnings a hundred times, so she turned off the television. The room was quiet. Comforted by the progress of the day and the knowledge that her family was safe at home, Susan couldn't resist a quick nap. Monica came to get Susan for the late evening visit, but she was in such a deep sleep that the nurse decided to let her sleep.

Monica went by herself to check on Jack. He was wide awake; his progress seemed to be as rapid as the falling snow. She straightened a few things in his private room, refreshed his pitcher with water and ice and almost routinely asked if he would like a sip of water. She thought how silly her question, until she noticed Jack purposefully blink his eyes. She asked again. He blinked again—twice. Monica put a small towel under his chin and held the cup up to his lips. Very carefully she tipped it toward him. The water ran down his chin and onto the towel. She was beginning to think her assumption had been foolish when she noticed Jack trying to swallow. A bit less water ran down his chin as he slightly parted his lips and tentatively began to drink.

After about three swallows he blinked again and she pulled the cup away. She placed the cup back on the nightstand and wiped the water off of his face. As she was hanging the damp cloth on the towel rack, she heard Jack slowly whisper, "Thank you."

Monica smiled calmly, held his hand, and whispered, "You are welcome." But, she still couldn't believe it.

She recalled that his chart indicated he might never speak again. This was one of those moments that truly fueled her passion for her job. She couldn't wait to share the news with Susan.

She walked over to the nightstand and turned the little angel directly toward Jack. He didn't notice. He just returned Monica's smile.

What a miracle, she thought. It would be the first of many.

Chapter 12

Monica stopped by the nurses' station to update her patient's chart and then made a beeline for Jack's wife. Susan had been in such a deep sleep that she thought she was dreaming when Monica shared the latest developments with her. She was grateful to realize that what Monica said was real.

Monica cautioned her that there were no guarantees, but that every little step was a great thing.

Monica thought Jack might be asleep before the scheduled 10:00 p.m. visit so she decided to take Susan for an early visit. Susan wasted no time in shaking off her sleepy state.

She walked in and sat down next to Jack. His eyes were closed again—until he heard her voice. He did not speak, but when he opened his eyes, he smiled for the second time.

Susan glanced over at the nightstand and her teary eyes fell upon the angel for the first time. She looked at Jack and then back to Monica.

"So this is the little angel that Chip was telling me about," she said.

Monica just smiled.

Susan knew she would probably have to wait until the next day to hear Jack's voice. She didn't mind. She would wait forever.

Monica decided to leave them alone for a few minutes. Susan sat quietly with Jack, and the silence felt companionable rather than threatening.

Monica was gone for about thirty minutes, although it seemed much shorter. She had a feeling that Wednesday was going to be a busy day, but that this evening was the start of a slow, cold, blizzardy night. She found Susan an empty room on the floor and told her to try to get a good night's sleep.

It had been quite a day, and as the heavy snow continued to fall, what would prove to be a remarkable evening unfolded. But this was one story neither the weatherman nor the media anchors would ever tell.

It was after midnight. The snow was so heavy that no one was out and all was quiet in intensive care. Most of the night shift was stranded at home, but there was no shortage of manpower because the afternoon shift was going nowhere. One nurse kept the radio set to a twenty-four-hour news station. It seemed every weather report indicated significant accumulation. The total snowfall had risen above two feet and there was no end in sight.

Susan was sound asleep in room 534 at the opposite end of the hall. She had been so grateful for a real bed. The waiting room was empty and dark.

Jack had fallen asleep just after Susan left, only to reawaken at eleven o'clock, when Monica came in to change the bag on his feeding tube. He had slept for most of the day. Now, for the first time since the accident, he felt somewhat awake. He had no recollection of the accident and no idea of why he was in this hospital. He just knew he needed to be there. He thought of Susan, Chip, Bobby, and Katie. He felt lonely in the empty room.

He could see the window out of the left corner of his eye and the heavy snow continuing to fall. The whiteness almost made it seem like daytime. He even noticed a bright sort of glow shining in from the winter night.

His brain raced back to Chip's afternoon visit. He could still hear his son's voice meticulously describing the angel. How unlike Chip to notice such details, he thought. Ever so slowly, he turned his head to the right. The movement caused a fair amount of pain but he didn't stop. Before long, the window had disappeared from view and the nightstand had entered his field of vision. He kept turning until the angel was staring back at him, directly at eye level.

He stopped moving and focused. Each feature of the angel caught his attention and seemed to send him some sort of message. The simple abstract wings with their hint of rust. The beautiful, yet nondescript face. The outstretched arms. And then there was something Jack could only feel. A sense of calmness. A sense of patience. A sense of peace.

He enjoyed this feeling for a moment, then painfully began to turn his head back to the left until he was staring straight up at the ceiling. He closed his eyes and began to drift off again.

He didn't drift far before his mind started filling with different thoughts and memories. He was exhausted. Maybe it was the medicine.

He opened his eyes again. There wasn't a sound in the room. Outside, the sky was busy with falling snow.

Chapter 13

Although it was exactly midnight, he wasn't aware of this. He knew it wasn't summer, but had no idea what the date actually was. Suddenly he had the overwhelming realization that he needed to do more than just open his eyes: he needed to really wake up!

He thought he heard a sound from the nightstand on the right. He slowly turned his head once more. Everything was in its place. No sound. No movement. Nothing different. A phone, a blue pitcher, a matching plastic cup, and the nurse's wonderful gift. Nothing had changed.

Except, he noticed the angel's wings had turned a sparkling white.

The pain subsided as Jack suddenly thought he heard a voice in his silent room.

This is real.

He felt confused, and thought maybe it was his medication. But the first message came again.

No. This is real. I'm real. I'm your special angel.

Jack tried to close and open his eyes several times to recapture the vision of the simple, rusting wings. Each time, the sparkling white just got a bit brighter.

Jack, please don't close your eyes. You've had them closed for too long. Open your eyes to what's real. I'm here to wake you up. We'll visit many times and I'll help you heal. They'll tell you today that the return of your voice is a miracle. It is. And then they'll say you'll never walk again. But they're wrong. You'll be fine, in time. But that's not what's most important.

Jack closed his eyes again. Without speaking out loud, he found he could somehow communicate his thoughts directly to the angel. His first response was simple, "What do you mean?"

You'll see what I mean soon enough. We'll visit often.

About that moment, Monica quietly entered the room. She was surprised to see Jack awake, and even more surprised to see him staring at the angel. Jack wanted to speak when she said hello, but nothing would pass his lips. She walked to the side of the bed. He unknowingly looked to Monica and then back to the little angel. Monica looked down at the little angel and went to pick her up. Jack wanted to warn Monica not to touch her, but couldn't say a thing. Monica's motions toward the angel continued until she lifted the little figurine into her hands. She took a close look at it and smiled as she remembered how much she'd loved finding the little angel. She thought of little Sarah, and how thoughtful it was for her family to suggest buying these for her patients. She looked back at Jack and gently told him the story. He listened carefully. He wanted to know where his angel had come from.

Monica continued the story, telling Jack about a few of the first patients she had given an angel to. He continued to listen. He was interested in what Monica was saying, but also very relieved she wasn't leaving just yet. She paused for a moment, mentally reminiscing about some of the other patients.

Monica met his eyes and shared more of her thoughts on the angel. She concluded by noting that the rusty wings were her favorite part. As Jack looked from the angel to Monica and then back to the angel, he realized that she couldn't see the wings of sparkling white. Monica looked at Jack and asked if he liked the rusty wings. He couldn't speak. He just slowly blinked his eyes. She didn't see.

Monica casually put the angel back on the table, wished him a good night, and headed toward the door. About halfway, she remembered she wanted to double check Jack's intravenous drip bag. Confirming that everything was fine, she looked back at the angel. This time she adjusted the angel so that she was more directly facing Jack.

The door shut tightly behind her. Jack was left with the brightness from the falling snow and sparkles from the wings of an angel.

Jack couldn't sleep. He stared at the clock and, even though the movement was painful, he frequently looked over to the angel. No sound, no movement, no further messages. Until just after three o'clock.

As he looked at the angel, words began to fill his mind.

Jack, I have a lot to tell you, and it'll take some time. You don't need to keep looking at me every five minutes for another message. In fact, not all of the messages will come from me. Some will come from those who visit you. You'll leave the intensive care unit soon, so you'll start to see a lot of people.

Jack somehow knew he could trust the angel's messages, but wondered how he would ever know which messages to trust from others.

I'll let you know what you need to know.

Jack began to think he was losing his mind.

No, this is real.

Jack realized then that the angel could read his every thought.

That's right. But I'm not here to judge you. I'll just respond.

Jack had no idea how this was happening, but he felt a sense of peace. In his typical impatient style, however, he was ready to get on with it.

Sure enough, the angel shot back, *Not so fast. That's your problem: you race through life. I'll give you messages and confirm the messages of others at my pace, not yours. And my first message is that life's not a race. It's a journey. You'll come to see the difference. It'll change your perspective on all your relationships. Only the journey is real.*

"Whatever. How did I get here? I don't remember anything."

You landed yourself here.

"From the way my body feels, I must've been in a bad accident. How are the people in the other car? Was it my fault?"

There was no other car.

"Oh, good. So no one else was hurt?"

Well, the train conductor didn't feel too good.

"Train?"

The train that hit you.

Jack couldn't believe it. He was sure he'd never take that kind of risk.

You didn't really know the risk you were taking. The train from the left was not the problem. You had plenty of time. But you never looked to the right. There were two risks. But in your race to beat the train you only noticed one.

"I feel terrible."

Of course you do, but we'll come to that later.

"So I didn't see the real risk."

What you still don't see is that those trains were a gift.

"I've never met a train that was a gift."

That's because you're in a race, not on a journey. The trains let you stop for a moment.

"I suppose you think red traffic lights are cute little packages hanging from wire ribbons."

Correct! What's your rush?

"Life's busy," thought Jack in obvious irritation. "Talk about what's real. Busy is real. In our world today, busy is normal!"

If you wish it to be.

"Oh, so I should just sit around and be worthless?" Jack was beginning to resent the angel's smug assurance.

I didn't say that. You've just created a way of life that seems normal to you. You've developed it in your work, but now you practice it in every area of your life. Jack, life doesn't have to be a shopping spree or a sprint to the grave. That's your choice.

"Isn't everyone in this race?"

Not everyone has just been hit by a train.

Jack thought he picked up a hint of humor in the angel's tone. "So you're saying nothing bad happens to those who go slowly?"

I didn't say that. Jack, if you want to make the most of our time together, you need to quit being so defensive and stop trying to jump to the easiest conclusion.

"I see."

That's exactly what I'll help you do.

"See?"

Well, truly wake up. The speed of your life has put you to sleep. You're not living consciously. People on journeys are aware of what they're doing. They experience the same ups and downs as everyone else, but they have a different perspective on their lives.

"Do they try to beat trains and run yellow lights?"

Probably not. They're not in a hurry.

"Do they get anything done?"

They get what matters done.

"And how do they keep focused on what's important?"

They think about it at red lights!

Jack wanted to laugh, but the effort was physically painful.

We've got plenty of time, Jack.

"I think I'm glad you're here."

Jack stared up at the ceiling. He thought about the pressures of the global village and the new economy. He thought about the many things that had pushed him to run in the race. They were subtle. Little by little he'd gone from walking to jogging to running without ever noticing the change.

The door opened and Monica walked in. She looked a bit tired, but was as cheerful as ever. Jack's eyes had been closed while he thought. It was an activity he hadn't engaged in for a while.

He opened his eyes and watched her go about her business. She didn't seem to be in a hurry about anything. Nor did she miss a beat. As she turned toward the bed, she noticed he was awake. He noticed it was just after four o'clock. She looked over at his intravenous pouch.

"Jack, you're a slow eater! You need to hurry and finish up." She looked at him and smiled. "Just kidding, no need to rush. I'll be back in just a little while to hang up your breakfast."

He wanted to ask Monica if she stopped for yellow lights. Somehow, he already knew the answer. Monica smiled as she left the room.

Because no one else was around, Mike took the 8:00 a.m. visit. Jack was wide awake, although still a bit groggy from the pain medicine.

"Thanks for coming," he whispered.

"It's great to hear your voice," Mike said cheerfully. "When I heard what happened, I wanted to get here as quick as I could."

Jack didn't say much, but he enjoyed listening to Mike reminisce about their earlier days. It had been a simpler time and they had enjoyed every minute. Mike began to talk about how life had changed, and about the busyness of it all.

"But I've learned life's not just a ride to be taken. I've slowed down to come and see you, and I'm so glad I did."

Jack looked to the angel. He sensed Mike's genuine friendship, and remembered the angel had told him that messages would come from many places.

The loud noise startled both of them as the doctor came in the room, accidentally pushing the door too hard and slamming it against the wall.

He was a substitute and certainly seemed to be in a rush. He didn't pay any attention to Mike, but got right down to business with Jack. "It looks like you have shown quite an improvement in the last twenty-four hours," he said. Jack smiled.

"If this continues," said the doctor, "I think we'll soon be able to move you out of intensive care." The doctor added, "I hear you've been able to speak. That's a miracle. Unfortunately, the odds that you'll ever walk again are very low." Jack could see the desolate expression on Mike's face as his friend reacted.

Jack looked directly at Mike and replied, "Don't worry. I'll walk."

Mike smiled. The physician didn't.

The doctor went through his procedures and left quickly. As the door closed, Mike looked at Jack and simply said, "People to see, things to do."

Jack nodded, and they both smiled.

Susan had slept quite well through the night. She was grateful for the bed that Monica had allowed her to use. She couldn't believe that she'd slept until nine o'clock. She would have slept longer, but was awoken by Carl calling on the cell phone. The record three-foot snowfall had shut down the Chicago area. The kids were cheering in the background because there was no school and Jeanne was cooking bacon, eggs, and waffles. Susan was pleased that everyone was fine.

The efficient economics of managed care dictated that Jack be moved to a regular room by noon. Monica had stopped by close to the end of her shift. As she changed his feeding bag, she told him that he would probably be moving in the next twenty-four hours. He'd only just met Monica, but a sense of sadness washed over him when he realized she would no longer be his night nurse. However, she quickly informed him that he would be on her visit list until he checked out of the hospital.

He couldn't believe her spirit of service. He thought of so many people where he worked who just went through the motions. He knew he could look in the mirror and find one more.

It was a few minutes after one o'clock when Jack arrived in his new room and the staff brought in a lunch tray. He couldn't eat. Mike had gone back to the motel to make some quick calls, and Susan had settled in at Jack's bedside.

Jack was tired, but he had asked Susan to turn on the TV. He couldn't remember much of anything, but he knew he was out of touch with the world. Susan told him that wasn't such a bad thing, but he wanted to watch anyway. Susan tuned in to one of the financial networks.

She joked about the authoritative analyses of the reporters.

"They act like they are the experts and drivers of the economy. I wonder how many could even run a small business."

Jack found humor in her informal comments. They both noticed that one stock was analyzed three times in thirty minutes. Jack thought about the irony of instant information. He thought about how harmful it was for the market value of these companies to be analyzed every fifteen minutes. He began to realize the dilemmas of the modern CEO.

Jack looked to the angel. He'd insisted that she be put in his bed for the ride from room 573 to room 1104.

Now the angel rested on Jack's new nightstand. Her wings glittered more brightly than ever in the sunlight.

These values are illusions. They're normal, but they're not real.

Jack understood. He thought back to the surge of dot-coms in the late 1990s.

Picking up on Jack's thought, the angel responded, *A great example, but only the tip of the iceberg.*

It seemed to Jack that everything old was worthless these days. If it wasn't new and slick, it wasn't valuable.

Jack, slick *is a good word. Slick creates illusions beyond worth. Potential is a great thing to recognize, but it's not everything. And it often isn't real.*

Jack looked at Susan. She was focused on the television.

She doesn't see me yet, but she'll have the chance to hear about me from you. Susan will understand much of what you're learning.

"So what's real?" he asked silently.

Tragedies are real. They teach us lessons, if we're willing to learn.

The angel's remark triggered strong feelings in Jack about the laundry list of bad news that always left him anxious: 9/11, Enron, the collapse of Arthur Andersen—even distant threats like nuclear tension on the Indian subcontinent or scandals in the Catholic Church. Jack felt overwhelmed by the world and the challenge of his own recovery.

Jack, don't look for answers until you understand the questions. Yes, each of these events contain an opportunity to learn. But when you are in a hurry, you don't have a chance to discover the lessons.

Jack thought of the immediate urge to simply get back to normal.

In your hurry, you look for scapegoats and Band-Aid solutions. Not for real lessons.

"I suppose we're scared of the lessons."

Terrified.

"Why?"

We'll get to that later. The problem is that each of these tragedies is a wake-up call. But you and most others are seduced into the comfort of your life. So you hit the snooze button.

Jack could relate to that metaphor.

The snooze . . . again and again.

Jack thought about how he loathed alarm clocks. He thought the snooze button was the greatest invention in the world. He looked over at Susan. He knew that she hated hitting the snooze button. Maybe she was better at seeing through the tragedies to the lessons.

Jack, you must wake up—and help others to wake up as well.

Jack was overwhelmed at this thought. He was also over-whelmed at the thought of his own recovery. He trusted his angel's insight into his physical rehabilitation, but he knew that the road to recovery would happen one step at a time.

Maybe that will be your greatest lesson.

Susan looked over at Jack who appeared to be simply staring at the ceiling. She walked over to him.

"Jack," she said. "How do you feel?"

"I feel better, much better."

Susan was afraid he would get overconfident about the timing of his recovery. Softly, she said, "Your recovery will take a while."

Jack looked into Susan's eyes. "I'm in no hurry."

Susan was surprised, but relieved. "So what's going through your mind?"

Without thinking, Jack replied, "Putting my life into perspective."

Jack, tell her you're looking for lessons.

"I'm looking for lessons."

This took Susan by surprise. "Lessons about what? Your accident?"

Jack thought for a moment. "I'm looking for the common threads of many lessons. It's been quite a year. We've had many teachers, but we still need some answers."

Susan knew something in her husband had shifted. Jack was thinking differently.

Jack, don't look for answers until you understand the questions.

"Susan, I'm so sorry about this accident," Jack said. Tears began to run down Susan's cheeks. He went on. "I hate what it's done to others. But this experience won't be in vain. I won't miss the lesson."

Susan was quick to comfort him. "Jack, we all have a lot to learn."

I told you she would understand.

"Susan," Jack replied, "please help me to learn."

Just then, a member of the staff he didn't know walked through the door.

"Jack, I'm Sheila, and I'll be taking you to physical therapy. Your first session will be tomorrow morning. I advise you to get plenty of rest. We'll be working against the odds."

Not everyone involved in the process of rehabilitation will be an angel.

As he looked at the rushed therapist, he replied, "I hear you."

The therapist gave a grimace of a smile and nodded as if to say, "I'm glad you understand." But Jack hadn't meant his reply for her alone. Sheila turned around and walked out.

Jack, remember you can learn from everyone, even those who appear to have the wrong perspective.

It would be a long road ahead, with many hills and valleys. Jack had no idea that the cure or the journey could be more challenging than the numb, frantic race he'd been running. But he was about to find out.

The temperatures had been falling all day. The snow had stopped and the skies had cleared. The sun was bright on the mounds of snow. The roads were quickly being cleared, but the forecast was dismal: an overnight low of twenty-five degrees below zero. No one even wanted to think about the wind chill.

Monica stopped by on her way to report for early duty in the intensive care unit. She was pleased to see everyone visiting Jack. All three kids, Susan, and both grandparents were crowded into Jack's private room. Jack had been enjoying the company but had fallen asleep after a while.

Chip took this opportunity to introduce Monica to Bobby, Katie, and his grandma, and to show them the angel. Monica blushed and smiled as Chip spoke.

"She brought this gift to Dad."

Only Jack truly knew the value of the gift. Monica chatted with everyone for a few minutes and promised to stop by a couple of times during her shift.

"What a joy to meet all of you," she said, giving each member of the family a hug before departing for the fifth floor.

The phone rang and Susan quickly answered. It was Mike. He told her that because Jack was improving at such a fast rate, he'd decided that he would head back to Memphis the following day. He convinced Susan to take a night off and go home while he stayed with Jack for a last night. Susan was pleased at the thought of returning home for the first time since the police had arrived to escort her to the hospital last Sunday morning.

Chip, Bobby, and Katie were equally thrilled that their mom was coming home. They continued to visit with each other while Jack lay quietly in bed resting his eyes and listening to the conversation.

Listen to your children. Don't ignore them.

Jack listened quietly. They all assumed he was asleep. It was a gift, however, to hear their words of love and encouragement. He'd never known how much he meant to each of them and he cherished the moment. Each word of their discussion was like a present on Christmas morning. He wondered why they didn't have these discussions more often. Maybe they did.

Quickly their words faded into the pictures of his dream. He was sitting in the front row of a college classroom. He was alone in the large amphitheatre—except for the professor. She had a pointer in her right hand and the wings of an angel.

Please watch carefully.

The lights went down and a huge white screen slowly descended from the ceiling. He waited patiently.

"Excuse me. I'm confused. I thought I had already graduated. What class am I in? I don't remember signing up for this. Is it required?"

You never graduate. That is the problem. We think we have finished when we are just beginning.

He watched as the crystal-clear video projected in amazing 3-D.

It was a replay of the life lessons that had passed unnoticed in the previous months. This time he wasn't too busy to watch and absorb their impact.

Please know that the lessons are not in the tragedy. The lessons are in what you take from them.

Jack could see that there was a lot to learn. He wondered what he could discover in examining each of the events. He looked for some common threads. He even tried to find what he didn't want to see.

The reel played over and over again. He saw the mistakes of others and at times felt judgmental. He saw carelessness, greed, selfishness, pride, ego, arrogance, and manipulation. He'd never noticed how deceit could put such an attractive façade on so many wrongs. He was amazed how speed could blur reality, and at how illusions could become so familiar that they became normal. Almost real. He watched with great interest—until he found himself in the middle of the picture driving a car on a cold and dark morning. The train was coming from the left . . . He looked to the right and broke into a cold sweat.

Susan quickly jumped to Jack's bedside and tried to wake him as sweat poured from his forehead and he repeatedly slurred the words, "How could I? How could I?"

He opened his eyes to see those he loved most dearly surrounding his bed.

Jack, you need to put your life into perspective now, but you must also look forward.

"How could I?"

There was not a dry eye in the room. Everyone realized that Jack's biggest hurdle would be to forgive himself. He looked at every one of them and whispered to each of them in turn, "I'm sorry, I'm so sorry."

No one said a word. They just stood around the bed, their hands softly touching his arms and legs, sending a reply of love.

Susan could see that Jack was exhausted. She began packing her things to leave. Suddenly, a knock at the door startled them. A young, thin stranger slowly opened the door and asked permission to enter. He looked tentative.

"Is this Jack Turner's room?" he asked.

Looking a bit puzzled, Susan said, "Why, yes, it is."

He walked over to Jack's bed with noticeable hesitation, as if he were a kid being forced toward a dentist's chair.

"My name's Tim," he said. "I was the conductor on the train that hit you. Real sorry to be meeting you under these circumstances." He reached out his calloused hand for Jack's.

"Me too," Jack quietly responded. He noticed that Tim couldn't have been more than twenty-five; much younger than he'd expected a train conductor to be.

"You know," said Tim, "I can't tell you how many times I've made fun of all the yahoos that try to beat us across the tracks. But this is my first accident. And now that it's happened, it's really shaken me up. I saw you. I saw you looking the other way. You got blindsided, and there was nothing I could do." Tim wouldn't look Jack in the eyes as he spoke. "I got blindsided, too. When my train finally stopped, I just closed my eyes. I said my first prayer in years."

Jack thought about the significance of what this young conductor had just told him. He wondered how to respond, when Tim continued. "Anyway, you don't need to hear me talk, but the reason I came by is that some of the guys and I took up a collection for you. It's not much, but maybe it'll help a little." Tim handed Susan the get-well card with the crew's contribution inside. Tim looked back at Jack, who mumbled something and smiled.

Tim said, "I'm so glad I was able to see you. And I'll check back again."

Susan thanked Tim for his visit and generosity. She said they were just on their way out, and Tim left the room with Susan and her family.

Jack was overwhelmed by Tim's visit. He realized how much his own behavior affected so many other people. For the first time, he felt a pang of guilt about the burden that his actions had now placed on others. Jack looked at the angel in desperation.

Jack, in order to make progress, the most critical step you'll have to take is to forgive yourself. It is in forgiving ourselves that we begin to see what is real. It is in seeing what is real that we can begin to make a positive difference. You work on forgiving yourself, and I'll help you see what's real.

Jack understood the angel. Though he tried to unravel the full meaning of her words, he was too weak to stay awake.

Jack slept most of the afternoon, and Mike arrived in the early winter darkness, just in time for Jack's dinner. Mike slowly and patiently helped Jack eat his first real meal. It didn't matter that Jack only ate a third; it was a start.

Mike read while Jack took a couple of brief naps. Jack insisted on turning out all the lights at ten o'clock so Mike could get a good night's sleep before his drive back to Memphis. Mike quickly fell asleep on his cot and Jack remained wide awake, staring into space.

It has been quite a day. We've taken some of the first and most important steps in our journey together.

"But I have a long way to go in forgiving myself for the pain I've caused others. I'm grateful for Tim. I'm grateful for my family. I'm grateful for Mike. They give me strength."

Forgiveness will come in time. What's rushed is not real. Remember, we're not in a hurry. You'll find forgiveness.

Jack, there are many people in the world who can't find forgiveness for themselves or others. Some think they're perfect, but no one's perfect. Some are lucky and have never had to pay for the consequences of their choices. How many drunk drivers have been blessed with a safe journey home? Their choice is no less wrong for going unpunished. How many CEOs or front-line employees have made bad business decisions but didn't destroy their business? Their choice is no less wrong. How many parents or teachers have unknowingly destroyed the true gifts of a child and never realized it? Their actions are no less wrong. I hate to tell you this, but if you had beaten that train on Sunday, your decision to rush would have been no less wrong.

Perfection is one of the illusions. And for many, it stands in the way of learning about forgiveness. Jack, you will learn a powerful lesson in forgiveness because you have suffered a serious consequence.

It's been a long day. Tomorrow will be a day of understanding. We'll begin by helping the medical staff here understand that you're going to walk again. Then we'll take a good look at what your work and your life mean to you. I'm going to ask you some pretty tough questions. I won't expect any answers, but I'll expect you to think about the questions.

"But when are you going to help me understand what I need to do? What good's understanding priorities, if I don't understand what I need to do?"

There you go, rushing again. We're in no hurry. You're not going anywhere soon.

"But can't we just start now? It's quiet and I'm not really tired. What about a sneak preview of what's to come?"

Good night, Jack.

"Good night."

Jack closed his eyes and quickly fell asleep. He would need all the rest he could get before the next day began.

Chapter 20

Mike had been up reading for two hours when Jack made his first movements around seven o'clock. The breakfast tray was delivered thirty minutes later. With Mike's assistance, Jack ate everything on his plate.

When Susan called, Mike insisted that he would stay until noon to give her plenty of time to arrive.

Sheila took Jack to physical therapy a few minutes after Mike hung up with Susan. The physical therapist proved to be respectful, but demanding. Jack tried to remind himself that it was all for his own good. He tried to fight off the unpleasant thoughts that crossed his mind. Jack wished he had put the angel in his robe, but then felt bad for thinking of her as a good luck charm.

The pain was almost unbearable at times, but he met the challenge in order to prove that he was determined and had every intention of walking again. Sheila was impressed with his perseverance. Jack decided by the end of the first session that he was going to like Sheila better than he had first assumed. The feeling was mutual.

He returned to his room shortly after ten o'clock and Mike was waiting for him. Jack wasn't looking forward to his friend's departure.

They talked about some of the emptiness of their business successes, but also of the opportunities it had given them. The two men quickly digressed into a few more remembrances of their younger years. They laughed until they cried and cried until they laughed. As they reflected on their earlier years, they thought about their hometown community and the deep and meaningful fabric of its culture.

Mike was the first to pause and reflect. "Jack, in our rush—yours and mine included—we've lost our true culture. At best, the economy has become our culture. Everything's about Wall Street and consumer confidence." Mike looked up to see if Jack thought he'd lost his mind.

"Jack," Mike continued, "sometimes I just stand out in my backyard and look up at the sky and wonder where we really are. And what our journey's truly about. We're about a simple moment in time. We've become experts at mechanics and processes and technology. But we've belittled the value of the heart. We're just these humans having an economic experience. I think our lives were meant to be far more than that. But when that effort absorbs all of our time and focus, we're left with little choice; after all, we become what we live day to day."

Mike had more to say: "I think of all the soldiers who fought for our freedom—not for our economic indulgence.

They fought for a purpose, not for an economic windfall. We live in a great country. That's because people fought and sacrificed for a purpose, not just to create an opportunity to get rich at any cost."

Jack looked from Mike to the angel and back. There was no intervention from the angel. Jack knew it wasn't needed.

Mike rose from his seat on the couch and walked over to the bed.

"Jack," he said, "our road ahead is not about simplification or some big vision, but about seeing our lives in a courageous new way. I'm not so sure if the 1990s were reliving the roaring '20s some seventy years later, or if we were living out a new version of the misguided ideas of the 1960s. But I think this addiction has evolved in spite of some pure motivations. It seems like good intentions don't always end up where you hoped they would."

"The question is," Mike continued, "whether we choose to wake up every now and then to see where we are and where we're headed. It means answering some tough, direct questions. I don't know if we'll like the answers. I see an obsession with wealth, work, and success. And no obsession is good."

Jack stopped listening long enough to ask, "Do you think there's really an addiction?"

Mike thought for a moment and then responded. "I know that addictions are hard to give up. I wonder how many people in business could give up what they have. I mean, walk away. Very few. Because they're addicted."

Jack's head was swimming. He hadn't really thought about it. He questioned his own ability to give up what he had. He looked at Mike and asked him if he could give up what he had.

Mike came back with a surprising answer. "I don't know. We're all part of this problem, and it's a cycle that's headed in an unhealthy direction."

"Don't get me wrong," he continued. "In our persistence, we've made some incredible strides towards better earthly conditions. But at what cost? I don't have the answers, and I know of only a few people who even want to ask the questions. I hope we can help each other sort through some of these issues."

Jack looked right back at Mike and said, "I'd like to do that. And I promise that I will. My accident is a tragedy, but I will not let this experience go by without gaining some insight."

Now there's an understatement. I'll share many insights with you. Mike has raised some important points and you'll be able to share some insights with him eventually.

There was a knock at the door. It was Susan.

Mike's departure was emotional. He promised to call when he arrived back in Memphis.

The hospital lunches were running late, but Jack's arrived by one o'clock. Susan helped him eat and then encouraged him to take a nap. She was wide awake after a night of uninterrupted sleep.

The second round of therapy that day would prove to be even more painful than the first. It took every ounce of physical energy that Jack had. He returned to his room exhausted but with good news: there was hope he would walk again. The angel had already promised him this, but Sheila's excitement for him was contagious.

Jack quickly dropped off to sleep after he got settled in bed again. Susan turned the volume on the television down low. The programs were mindless, but strangely, the commercials caught her attention. She normally used the remote to avoid the commercials, but for some reason she decided to watch each one of them this time. She was beginning to perceive the masterful illusion that was crafted through their subtle messages. Often, it seemed, the message had little to do with the product, but everything to do with slowly pulling you into needing what you want.

When Jack opened his eyes, she was mumbling to herself, "When is enough, enough?"

He looked at her. "What are you talking about?" He was still groggy and not sure if he was still dreaming.

Susan smiled. "I was just wondering when enough is enough."

A great question.

"It seems that we're never satisfied," Susan said. "Our whole mission is more."

Jack thought about his discussion with Mike about addiction.

Susan went on. "It's like we're nothing more than greyhounds chasing rabbits at the dog track. Always close, but never quite there."

It takes skill to succeed, but it also takes discipline and courage to be successful. What you get and gather is insignificant, for nothing is really yours.

Susan told Jack about her afternoon focus on commercials. Jack could hear the voices of his parents talking about the Great Depression. They had tried to impress upon him the deceit of advertisements and they often referred to Susan and Jack as members of the disposable society. Jack's dad talked about how their generation had used everything to its final drop. Nothing was thrown out. All was used, reused, converted, and squeezed to the last possible usage. Jack knew this was true. He would kid his parents about squeezing the last bit of toothpaste from the tube. It was an analogy he made repeatedly for everything his parents stretched.

Jack knew his generation was different. All their stuff was easy come, easy go. Leftovers were almost unheard of. Easy had overtaken necessary. Conservation and commitment had become old-fashioned words. Disposable was the way of life—and sometimes that habit also applied to mission, purpose, and relationships.

Susan and Jack talked about their own addiction to stuff.

Jack, you must understand that there is nothing wrong with nice things—unless they begin to control you. There are many rich people who are not addicted to anything and there are many poor people who are obsessed with getting everything. The amount is not the issue. The addiction is what's crucial.

"Susan," Jack asked, "have we become addicted?"

Susan had always prided herself on her simple tastes; this made it hard for her to face the question. After a long and thoughtful pause, she responded, "Yes, Jack, we're addicted."

But the addiction is not what I want you to see. It's the consequence.

Jack looked at Susan. "So what are the consequences?"

Susan paused to reflect. "Choices. It's about choices and their inevitable compounding effect."

Susan is right. The effect is subtle and therefore, you never see where you're really headed.

Susan loved the conveniences they had come to take for granted. She hadn't thought about what stood behind the façade that was the backdrop for their lives.

Addiction leads to consequence.

Jack couldn't bear to think about the consequence. He thought about work. He knew all too well the pressures of meeting Wall Street expectations. He had been thinking of the upcoming release of quarterly earnings on the way to work on Sunday morning. Everything and everyone centered on delivering those expectations.

Then Jack asked Susan, "How did we get here?"
She was silent.

And the angel replied to Jack, *Slowly.*

"How bad is it?" he asked the angel silently.

Getting worse.

Jack started thinking about his own financial portfolio. Either he or Susan checked their investment balances almost every weekend. Throughout the '90s, they couldn't believe how fast their wealth had increased—beyond their wildest imagination.

Look in the mirror if you want to see part of the problem. You sit in the silence of your expectations. Your actions voice your real choice, and your choice delivers the consequence.

Jack thought about how they had moved their investments around to stimulate growth. He thought of how their expectations had steadily risen. Normal returns were never good enough.

When is enough, enough?

"Jack," Susan said, breaking into his thoughts, "we don't like to think of ourselves as the problem, but we're as guilty as anyone."

Think about your mutual funds. Tell me the name of one company in which any of your funds are invested.

Jack was ashamed. He had no idea where his mutual funds were invested. If his investments had anything to do with his values, it was strictly by luck rather than intention. He wanted to share the guilt, so he posed the angel's question to Susan. She had no idea either.

Wake up.

It was an awakening, all right. And Jack had no problem mentally following the scenario through to its consequences. In his executive role in a public company, he lived out the pressures of those consequences. And helped enforce them on others.

Jack reflected on how corporate values displayed on a lobby wall really used to mean something. In those days, Jack knew there wasn't a major decision being made that wasn't analyzed symbolically for its adherence to company values. Everyone knew that the values ruled.

Values have become window dressing. They make great content for employee orientations, and every now and then they are paraded out as justification for some ill-conceived management need—often so that bottom-line expectations can be achieved in the short term. Real values are never about the short term. They're always about the long run. And, at times, they create some short-term discomfort.

"Susan," Jack said, "we've become allergic to discomfort. We'll avoid it at all costs. The bottom line's become everything, at work and at home."

It's become everything.

Jack continued. "We can try to fool ourselves, but the bottom line has become the end."

And not the means. Jack, do not be confused. The bottom line in any organization is critical, but only because it keeps the dream alive. If it becomes the focus and the spoken or unspoken mission, it will always deliver an empty promise. And it will lead to an insatiable hunger for more. Only a handful will have a passion for the bottom line, but all will become its slave.

"Susan," Jack insisted again, "we've become slaves to our material addictions."

She stood up and went to look out at the sun setting over the frozen winter horizon. She dwelled upon the great strides the nation and the world had made, thinking of all the advancements in medicine, science, technology. She wondered aloud how we all could have fallen prey to the most basic illusions.

Jack now knew the real reason he lay in this hospital bed. He was beginning to see past the surface of the situation and into the root causes. But after a few moments, he started to second-guess the entire conversation he'd just had with his wife.

Don't go back up to the surface.

"I need some air," Jack said.

Susan quickly turned from the window, concern in her eyes. She walked over to the bed. "What do you need?"

Jack looked up and smiled. "Never mind." He didn't realize he'd answered the angel out loud. He wished that Susan could experience the angel.

She will. For now, though, she'll experience me through you. You'll be the messenger. Just dive back below the surface.

Jack looked to Susan and delivered the rhetorical question, "So, how did we get here? Slowly."

With increasing speed. You have come to want so much. You have come to need what you want, instead of wanting what you need.

The dinner tray arrived. Jack didn't want much, but knew that he needed to eat.

Be careful of what you want. Your wants will define your habits. This is not good or bad. It's just a fact.

After dinner, Jack convinced Susan to go home to be with the kids and get another good night's sleep. Jack had every intention of sleeping himself.

Susan finally agreed, kissed him good night, and departed.

Jack closed his eyes, anticipating a need for lots of rest before his next physical therapy session.

Everything was fine—until the dream started.

All of the dignitaries of the world were in the audience: every president, every prince, and every CEO. Jack had been chosen as the business professor of the year. He felt inadequate and inferior—until he spoke his first word. Then he was overtaken with a sense of wisdom and confidence.

"We're failing in our mission. We're inadequate in our purpose." Jack looked out to the front row. Two CEOs rolled their eyes. Jack didn't care. He continued. "All of you will fail in each of your callings if you don't conquer your one biggest obstacle."

He paused and could sense the impatience. He heard a few jibes from the audience.

"Who are you to tell me about obstacles?" one man called out.

Jack chose to ignore him.

"Your biggest obstacle is your own success," Jack continued. "You have so much to lose. Most of you protect what you have at all costs. Some of you have come to think that you have a right to what you have earned. You sacrifice nothing. You want leadership, but you don't want to serve."

Finding his stride, he went on. "Unfortunately, you teach all of your followers by your example. You train them, not through the words of your carefully orchestrated speeches, but through your actions and decisions. You speak from both sides of your mouth. You embrace historic values while demanding unrealistic bottom-line advancements."

Pointedly, Jack added, "You've been seduced to this place by your own success. And each step of the way you've lost a piece of your courage. You have become the follower. And many of you have become the prisoners of your own addictions."

Jack looked out to the audience. There was silence. Dead silence. He didn't know if the stares were piercing him or supporting him. But he felt a sense of peace. You could have heard a pin drop.

Until someone yelled, "How do you know all this?"

Jack paused to gather his thoughts and then responded, "Because I looked in the mirror. And I woke up to what I didn't want to see. When I look out at you, I see a reflection of me."

The room began to spin. Jack felt sick. He woke up in a cold sweat. Monica was standing at his side.

"Jack, are you okay?"

He couldn't respond. He couldn't speak. His legs were numb. And his heart was pounding. But he could turn his head to the right.

He looked over to the nightstand. The angel was gone.

Monica looked around for the angel as she sensed the emptiness in Jack. She too was sad. Where could the angel be? Monica promised Jack that she would ask the other nurses and check at the nurses' station. She knew that it was unlikely that a doctor or a nurse would ever remove anything from a patient's room, but she promised to ask anyway.

It was a nice surprise to see Monica, but once she left, Jack couldn't get the angel out of his mind. He tried to quash his disappointment. After all, it was just a little figurine.

Jack stared up at the ceiling through the early-morning hours until his breakfast arrived. He wasn't very hungry as he pondered the conversations of the last few days. He thought about the illusions people create. This reminded him of a quote he had recently heard: "Life is simply chaos covered by a thin veneer of order."

He began to see past the veneer. Everyone wanted their due. It wasn't about what you needed, but about what you proved to others you could get.

He kept thinking about how people wanted it all and wanted it now. And he knew many were prepared to believe in false hopes to obtain these things. He felt sad that human beings, while becoming so advanced, had still remained so primitive.

Where was his angel? He had plenty of questions and he was getting quite hungry for some real answers.

Jack continued to stare at the ceiling and wallow in his circumstances. He thought of how he had tried to master all the relevant leadership skills, but it had all been for a leadership façade. He was hungry for substance. He had mastered skills, yet become ignorant in his heart. He smiled as he thought of a few CEOs he knew who truly had substance. Now there was depth and passion and purpose. But the list was short. Most had fallen into the bottom-line trap of the short-term. They felt compelled. They had too much to lose, and they had lost sight of their roles as servants. As he felt his anger mounting, he wondered if he was being too hard on them. Probably. He thought of the pressures that pushed them there. He thought back to the expectations of Wall Street. Day traders. Greedy investors. Hungry gamblers. Maybe the CEOs simply had become the pawns in a game that was headed down a dark road. A dead end.

What really disappointed him was the fact that he had volunteered to play along in the game. He'd lost the courage required to make a difference.

He needed some real answers. But there were none. The angel was gone.

Susan arrived just in time to convince him to eat before his food turned cold. While he ate, he asked her some of the questions he wanted to ask the angel. It felt overwhelming. Neither of them had answers, but they no longer felt like ignoring the questions. It was time to search for truth and not for the next convenience.

Sheila knocked at the door. Jack was reminded that anything worth accomplishing was going to be a challenge. For the first time, he knew real recovery was not about changing the world; rather, it was about changing himself. Courage would help him walk, and that same courage would help him find some answers.

He was ready to accept the pain.

Jeanne arrived just after the midday meal. Jack had not eaten anything for lunch and was sound asleep upon her arrival. He slept well, but eventually woke up as his fever started to climb again. By midafternoon he was burning up. The doctors were concerned and took all the necessary precautions.

Jack seemed to go from one extreme to the other that afternoon—first burning up and then freezing. He was pleased that Susan and her mother were there, but he felt lonely without the angel. She had become his mental anchor in this storm.

Monica was working a double shift and had stopped by on the way to her duties in intensive care. She told him that there was no trace of the angel, but said that she had already called to get a replacement. After she left, Jack realized how much he looked forward to Monica's visits. He was beginning to comprehend her commitment to selfless service.

By late afternoon, Jack's fever had abated somewhat. He told Susan about some of the thoughts that had disturbed him earlier. Jeanne just listened. She was quite a lady. Susan was her youngest child and had been a bit of a surprise, so her mother had been older than the average new mother. She had a great memory and quite a frame of reference. She often talked about the Depression of the 1930s. She had been a young girl then, but she still had vivid memories of her family's struggles.

Jack had never asked her about the details. They seemed to have little relevance to him. But something today intrigued him about that snapshot of time and he was finding the energy to ask some questions. Jeanne was more than happy to share her reflections. As she reminisced about a difficult but far simpler time, Jack enjoyed listening.

While he listened, he noted that he and Susan also had stress and pressures. They were different, but they were real, for they were relative to the times. Susan laughed as her mother described their amazement at the ability to send instant information on the telegraph. Jack asked how many telegraphs they would send a day. He laughed when she responded matter-of-factly that they were swamped if they had more than two a day.

Susan looked at Jack and thought of e-mail. Jack was usually on the cutting edge of any new technology. But with these advantages came some undetected and profound consequences. The consequence of this increase in speed had been subtle but profound.

As they continued to talk about leaps in communication technology, Jack experienced a renewed sense of emptiness. Although they were still relatively young, Susan and Jack were starting to feel quite old. Were they simply reaching back for the "good old days" or were they beginning to see something that everyone else was missing?

Jeanne had seen it all and she wondered where things were headed.

Susan responded without hesitation. "You may be the only person asking this question. I'm not so sure anyone really cares, as long as their comfortable life isn't affected. I've certainly shared that mind-set. What else can you do?"

Jack searched for a real answer to her question, but to no avail. He looked at the nightstand to see the empty space reserved in his mind for his angel. He was desperate for some answers, or at least some guidelines. But the angel was still missing and the questions still had no answers.

Jack closed his eyes. It all seemed so overwhelming.

Finally, he decided he was hungry, and Susan helped him eat. Jack had only taken two bites before the deafening explosion created a blinding darkness.

Chapter 24

The hospital's emergency power came on immediately, but it was clear that there was a huge problem. The dim light under the door barely penetrated the complete blackness in room 1104. Susan made her way to the window to see if she could figure out what had happened. As she opened the heavy drapes, she could see a tower of orange flames rising from what appeared to be a gasoline truck.

Seconds later, the door swung open. Carl and the kids had just gotten off the elevator on the eleventh floor when they heard the explosion. Katie ran to her mom, grabbed her, and started crying. Everyone wondered what would happen next.

As Susan continued to look out the window with Katie at her side, she saw lots of emergency vehicles arriving.

The sound of sirens outside and complete silence inside were interrupted when Chip stumbled over his own feet trying to get to the side of the bed to sit with his dad. As he reached for the side sink, a few things went flying off the counter and onto the floor. Everyone but Chip burst into nervous laughter.

After Chip regained his balance, he sat down next to his dad. Jack grabbed his hand.

"Chip, are you okay?"

"Chip, if you think you can make it, I just remembered they told me there's a small flashlight in the top drawer of this nightstand. Why don't you check it out?" Jack asked. "If you find it, use it to pick up whatever went crashing."

Chip found the flashlight in the drawer. He turned it on and went about the business of picking everything up while everyone else but Jack stared out the window.

Chip only discovered a couple items on the floor. He picked those up and put them back on the sink counter. Then he decided to look under the nightstand and the bed. The floor under the nightstand was clean and clear. As he moved his flashlight to the right he saw something under the bed, but couldn't tell what he was looking at. He straightened his body, slid under the mechanical framework of the hospital bed, and reached until he grabbed the object and then crawled out from under the bed.

He pointed the flashlight at the object in his hand, and held it out to Jack, who was drifting off to sleep.

"Hey, Dad, what was your angel doing under the bed?"

Jack opened his eyes with a start.

Chapter 25

Jack couldn't believe it. He found it hard to hide an excitement that only he would understand.

"Chip, thank you for finding her! I was so sorry that she was missing."

Chip put the unscathed angel back on the empty corner of the nightstand and turned her to face his dad. He sat back on the bed and turned off the flashlight. Jack looked over and smiled as he noticed the angel's sparkling white wings. They shined brighter than ever in the darkness.

Everyone in room 1104 was pleased when the electricity was restored within the next hour. Nevertheless, they were tired, and decided to pack up and head home so that Jack could get a good night's rest.

He hated to see them go and looked forward to their visit the next day. But he was not about to go to sleep. His angel was back and he was ready for some answers.

After the good-bye kisses and hugs, the family was quickly out the door. No sooner had the door closed than

Jack looked directly at the angel, who was looking directly back at him.

"And how might you have fallen under the bed?"

You're always looking for answers to everything. Once again, you've caused your own problem.

That was the last thing he needed to hear.

During your dream you flung out your hand and sent me flying so hard against the front of the sink counter that I hit it and bounced to the floor and under the bed.

Jack remembered his dream. He did have a habit of flinging his hands and arms in his sleep.

But don't worry. Flying around doesn't hurt me.

He didn't appreciate the angel's gentle humor. Jack was in no mood for it. But he was relieved that she was back in his sight.

"So why didn't you tell me where you were? Poor Monica's already ordered a replacement for you."

That's because you're going to need that so-called replacement later. All part of the plan, you see.

"But why didn't you help me from under the bed? You knew I had lots of questions."

Of course I did. But you are in too much of a hurry for answers. Today was a day for questions. And you and Susan did a fine job of searching for them.

"So . . . what about answers?"

Soon. Very soon. I'm not sure you'll like all the answers, but I think you'll find the journey meaningful.

A peacefulness settled over Jack. He grew sleepy and before long fell into a deep sleep.

His angel was back and now no one was in a hurry.

Chapter 26

The explosion of the gasoline truck left a blackened area on the front lawn of the hospital, violating the otherwise pristine white winter scene. By the time Jack awoke, the last few inches of fresh snow had covered the blemish.

It was quiet this Saturday morning. Jack had slept through Monica's two visits in the middle of her night shift. Her first visit was just after midnight. She was surprised, but pleased, to see the original angel sitting on Jack's nightstand. Nevertheless, she placed a small package containing a new angel at the foot of his bed.

When Monica stopped by Jack's room on her way out of the hospital at 7:15 in the morning, Jack was wide awake and hungry. Happily for Jack, the staff delivered his breakfast tray while Monica was with him. She helped him prepare his breakfast just the way he liked it as he told her about Chip's discovery of the angel during last night's crisis in front of the hospital.

"Then I guess you won't be needing this new angel," Monica said, pointing to the package she'd left in the night.

"Thanks," Jack replied, "but I'm pleased with what I have."

Jack, listen to these words. This mind-set is foreign to you and most others.

Monica smiled at Jack. She continued helping him with his breakfast. When she finished, Monica wished him a wonderful day and left with the extra angel tucked in her arm.

Jack knew Susan would be arriving soon. He looked over at his beloved angel.

I sensed your frustration yesterday.

"So you were listening under the bed."

Of course.

"Yes, you're right. I do get frustrated."

But don't deceive yourself. Even though the frantic pace of life can cloud your thinking with superficial sound bites, you always have a choice about what you accept. Be careful not to blame others for your lack of responsible thinking.

Jack knew the angel was right. He had enough problems without trying to pass the blame around. And the projection of his own irresponsible persuasions onto others was only the beginning of his personal issues.

Jack, you'll soon find that your accident is a gift. The accident itself was hardly a blessing, but what you choose to do with the aftermath can be. You have started to scratch the surface. But you're still searching for some easy magical answer. Life's not about answers. Life's about discovery. And to truly discover, you must begin to dig deeply. Little in life is what it initially appears to be.

"What do you mean by that? Sometimes you confuse me and other times you scare me."

There's nothing to be scared about. You just have to be willing to dig. Most people don't dig, because they are afraid of what they will discover. So they choose to live, work, play, and problem-solve on the surface for a quick-fix alternative. I'm surprised there are any Band-Aids left in the world. There is no progress unless you dig for the roots.

What you must discover is quite simple. The road to get there may take time. The issues we face are much like a cancer: complicated and invasive. They're difficult to find and manage, for they live among us. And often they live within us.

The real issues can be hidden for only so long. Eventually the root of the weed begins to sprout, each time thicker and more intrusive.

"So why do we resist the dig?"

That's simple. Because the treatment is sometimes more painful than the disease itself. And because you like what is normal. The problem is that what appears to be normal isn't always real.

"You're not making sense."

That's because you're still standing on the surface.

Jack pinched himself. Was he asleep or awake? Was this even real . . . or was it a dream? He looked at his dependable travel alarm. It was 8:15 a.m., he was awake, and Susan was entering the door.

S usan pulled out her pocket calendar to try to figure out how she was going to manage when her parents returned to their home in the next few days. She started to think out loud.

Jack felt a growing sense of pain and responsibility for her more complicated daily schedule. As he listened, he sensed a deeper sorrow at work in his soul as Susan mindlessly verbalized the increasingly complicated list of chores and activities.

As you dig, do not find problems in every morsel of dirt. The problem is not the dirt, it is the motives of the digger.

Susan kept shuffling her calendar, trying to make things fit. Jack kept shuffling his thoughts, trying to make sense of it all. What had seemed so normal and critical only six days before now seemed to take on a totally different significance.

Keep digging. You'll begin to see that no one's isolated from the problem. You'll see that everyone's attached to the roots.

Jack looked across the room to the small ledge that ran the length of one wall. Over the week it had slowly been filled with beautiful arrangements of flowers from many well-wishers. He looked to the far right end of the ledge where for the first time he noticed a small American flag sitting in a black plastic holder. The flag had been placed in his room and every other room of the hospital just weeks after the September 11 terrorist attack on the United States.

As he looked at the flag, he thought of what he had come to take for granted as his blessed American way of life. During his lifetime, he had lived through unprecedented change in his country. But where was this growth headed? As he mentally began to dig deeper, he wondered.

Don't garden too quickly. If you do, you'll pull the flowers with the weeds. And don't be deceived; every great strength or blessing can become a weakness. Don't be so naïve that you miss the point in the fact that every great nation in history has fallen. Every single one. Each had so much to lose that no one wanted to dig deep enough to find the real enemy. It's never too late. In fact, there's never been a greater time for hope. It's not important what we face; what matters is how we respond.

Jack knew the angel was right. As Susan completed making all the arrangements for the next week using her laptop and cell phone, Jack realized his physical recovery was only the beginning and that he was not the only one who needed to recover.

Promptly at nine o'clock, Sheila entered to take Jack to physical therapy. He wasn't looking forward to this session. Jack felt physical pain as he was helped into a wheelchair. He glanced at his angel for encouragement and strength.

Just remember: the cure can be more painful than the problem. The long-term issue becomes which you are more willing to endure.

The last day of his first week in the hospital seemed to drag on forever. The therapist's report indicated some improvement. Susan left just after Jack returned from his afternoon physical therapy session. He was exhausted, both mentally and physically. Although he had insisted that everyone stay at home on Saturday night, he felt quite lonely in his hospital bed. He had his angel, but there had been no response from her since morning. It wasn't for lack of his continued thinking, for even through the pain of therapy he continued to dig.

As the January sun was setting on the beautiful snow, his room became dark. He didn't move to turn on the lights. He simply enjoyed the fading light. He was soon sound asleep.

The crash of the dinner tray ripped his eyes open. The room had settled into total darkness, except for the small indicator lights of the medical equipment remaining by his bed. A hospital staff member in a candy-striped uniform flipped on the light and mumbled her apologies through her embarrassment.

Jack smiled back with a simple response. "No problem." Now awake, his hopefulness temporarily crashed along with the dishes. He was pulled back to reality.

A couple of maintenance staff came to clean up the scattered mess. He was given a new dinner tray and soon enough he slipped back into a lonely Saturday night.

Jack began to slowly look around the room.

What do you see?

He began to notice every detail: the drapes, the equipment, the shiny floor in the far corner. He thought about the care that he'd received during the past week. His eyes slowly passed the far ledge, noticing every single flower arrangement and pausing to clearly think about each sender. His loneliness began to slowly fade.

Continue to dig.

Jack began to examine and question all that he'd become. He began to dissect the subtle choices and the circumstances that had evolved in his life. He began to realize that nothing could be assumed. Nothing could be taken for granted. He began to feel cautiously hopeful again. At that moment he began to hear familiar laughter outside his door.

The door opened and with a flick of a switch, all the lights in his room came on. Katie was the first to appear around the corner, then Bobby, followed by Chip. Susan walked in behind both of her parents. They were only the beginning. It seemed like the flow of the parade into his room would simply never end, from neighbors to coworkers to friends from his church. The room was soon filled to capacity with people. He couldn't believe his eyes. His throat began to tighten, his lips began to quiver, and his eyes filled with tears. He'd never been thrown a surprise party—and what a time for his first! As he looked around, he saw his everyday angels. He'd never seen them in this light before.

This is no dream. You're surrounded by love. But it's a love that becomes invisible in the speed of life. You've only started to slow down. You've only begun to dig. And what you'll find will go far beyond your expectations. Don't be afraid. If you dig, you'll find miracles. But first you must find trust. It won't try to find you. It'll be worth your time. Jack, as you dig, you won't be the only one to discover what you find. Others will benefit. Look around.

Jack gazed around the room. There was no idle surface chatter. Instead, there was silence. He looked around at each of them. He reached for Chip's and Katie's hands on one side and Bobby's on the other, whispering, "Thank you."

He was surrounded by love. It was here that he could begin.

Chapter 29

It had been close to an hour since everyone had departed. Jack was no longer tired, but he was emotionally drained. Yet for the first time in this whole experience, he felt a real sense of hope and courage.

Monica walked in, grinning ear to ear. Jack couldn't believe he had known her for only a week. He felt as close to her as if she were a friend from childhood.

"Jack," she said, "I'm in a bit of a rush. Things are unusually busy in intensive care tonight, but I just wanted to bring you this package. It's addressed to you with no return address. It showed up in our afternoon mail delivery. Do you have any idea who might have sent it to you?"

Jack took the medium-size package and examined it. "I have no idea. I assume it's safe to open!"

Monica smiled. "I'm sure it'll be fine. It's likely a gift from someone who cares about you. I hope you enjoy it. I'd better run now."

Jack tore into the package as soon as Monica departed. Inside the box was a bright white envelope. He pulled it out and read the note preprinted on the front:

Don't open this envelope until instructed to do so.

The note reminded him of the standardized tests he took in school. They always started with a blank page, except for the simple instruction: "Do not turn the page until told to do so." But this time there was no teacher watching. In fact, no one at all was watching. He was ready to rip into the package—and then glanced at the angel.

Don't even think about it! You must wait.

"Oh, so you arranged this."

Of course.

"So what are we waiting for?"

Patience. It's the unwritten lesson of this package. You'll have a chance to practice it.

"Do I have to?"

It's not that you have to; it's that you need to.

"I've been practicing patience all week, waiting for answers while you insisted that I focus on questions."

You've done quite well. But patience is not only about waiting; it's also about your attitude toward the wait. Remember, we're in no rush.

"So this package finally contains the answers."

I wouldn't call them answers. Life's not about answers. At best they'll guide you to a new foundation from which you can rebuild, if you choose.

"Okay, so I choose. When do I start?"

Soon. Jack, no one here can tell you how long your hospital stay will be. As this week progresses, you will be increasingly ready to get out of this place. If you were to ask your doctor and therapists, you'd likely get mixed messages. Let me help you. You'll go home when we're done.

"And when might that be?"

You're always looking for an answer! But this time I'll give you one. Tomorrow is Day One.

Inside this package you will find twelve envelopes. One for each of the days you'll remain here. Each envelope is numbered on the outside. You'll open one envelope each day. That's the easy part. And what they contain will seem easy, but don't be confused by their simplicity. They're quite complex. You can share each opened card with others. The real messages are contained in their insights.

"So does that mean I go home on the twelfth day?"

You're getting ahead of yourself. But that's correct.

"So can I open one now?"

Yes, you can open the big white envelope.

Jack carefully opened the envelope and, just as the angel promised, there were twelve yellow numbered envelopes inside. He pulled them out and put them in order. He sat them by his side and slowly picked up the envelope marked with the number one.

Patience, my friend. Not so fast.

"You mean I can't start yet?"

That's right. Remember, tomorrow's Day One.

Jack looked at the clock. It was ten o'clock. He smiled and teased the angel, "You know, tomorrow begins in less than two hours."

You're so technical.

Jack reached for his travel clock and set the alarm for midnight.

"Don't mistake my enthusiasm for impatience," he quipped.

Never.

Jack turned the radio dial to his favorite jazz station, pushed the bedside control to turn off the lights, and soon fell asleep.

The alarm was startling. Jack's eyes flew open. For the first time in years, Jack didn't hit the snooze button. He focused his eyes on the clock face—midnight! Then, looking past the bright green display, Jack saw a tiny pair of small, white, glittering wings.

Welcome to a new day and a new week. You may begin.

He turned on the small light above his bed and squinted at the yellow envelope on top. He checked the number to confirm he had the first card. He looked at the big black number one on the front and then looked over to his angel for confirmation.

What are you waiting for?

"Patience!" Jack opened the envelope and removed the enclosed greeting card. On the cover he read:

God is in control.

He opened the card and read the single word:

Chapter 30

Always.

Jack was taken aback. He thought how often his ego had gotten in the way at work, at home, and with friends. He remembered the definition of ego he'd read in a book by Ken Blanchard: "to Edge God Out." He knew he'd done that a lot. Not intentionally, but through his choices and actions. Often he had just relied on his skills and talent. He forgot they were not of his own making, but gifts from God.

This is the most important message that you'll read. If you miss this one, none of the others really matter. It's easy to forget and begin to believe your successes are your own doing. That may be the greatest problem in the world today.

Jack had often seen the impact of ego in the actions of others, but rarely chose to look at himself in the same light.

It seemed to be a common theme these days. Freedom of speech meant freedom for everyone but God. There was no place for God in schools, businesses, or government. And Jack followed the rules. He didn't speak of God, and over time didn't even think of God.

So, Jack thought, it shouldn't come as a surprise that we've lost sight of who's really in control.

Jack knew that relinquishing control would take more than a single day. It would be hard for him, because it flew in the face of his intellect and his sense of taking ownership of his own life.

Don't be confused. God is in control, but He fully expects you to take responsibility for your life.

Jack, remember, "This is the day the Lord has made. Let us rejoice and be glad in it." This is true today, tomorrow, and every day to come.

Jack looked up at the ceiling and closed his eyes. He quietly lay on his back, thinking of how he could give his life back to God. He knew it would take faith and courage. He wanted to do it, but wondered if he would.

For the first time in a long time, Jack began to pray. He knew that he couldn't change his life on his own. He'd need some help. And so he prayed for help and then quickly slipped into a deep sleep.

Susan quietly entered Jack's room. Outside the snow was still piled high beneath a bright blue sky. She had decided to surprise Jack with her early arrival and a dozen glazed donuts. She knew they were his favorite.

He was sound asleep as she tiptoed over to the ledge in front of the window. First she put the box of warm donuts on the ledge. Next she placed her purse and a big cloth beach bag on the overstuffed brown sleeper chair.

She took the bright red plate from the plastic bag hanging from her arm and read the words that circled its rim, moving her lips in silence.

"You are special today."

She looked at the plate and thought of the many times they had used it for birthdays and other special occasions. She looked at Jack, peacefully sleeping, and knew these words had more meaning today than ever before.

Susan opened the box and put two of the glazed donuts on the plate. She then pulled a yellow carnation from one of the flower arrangements, breaking the stem about eight inches below the bloom. She took the plate and the flower and put them on the cart next to Jack's bed.

It was then that she noticed the yellow envelope and the greeting card by Jack's hand. Susan wondered who'd sent it. She picked up the card and read the words on the front:

God is in control.

Then she opened the card and read the inside verse:

Always.

She noticed the collection of sealed envelopes on the nightstand by the angel, but continued to ready her breakfast surprise for Jack. As a last-minute thought, she added the card to the tray with the front facing him. When she finished, she leaned over and kissed Jack on the forehead.

He slowly opened his eyes. With the winter sun just rising and reflecting off the frozen snow, Jack squinted at the brightness as he focused on Susan's smile. Their eyes met briefly. Then Jack looked toward the sweet smell of warm donuts on his breakfast tray. He saw the two donuts, the red plate, and the yellow carnation. He smiled and then noticed the card.

God is in control.

Maybe giving up control wasn't so bad.

"I see you found my card," he said.

Susan smiled. "Yes, and I like it. I see you've got a bunch of cards. Who sent them?"

Still sleepy and a bit foggy, Jack said, "I'm not quite sure."

It's all right, you can tell her they're from me. You can even tell her about me.

Jack closed his eyes for a moment, wondering where to begin. Wondering if he could make sense of it all.

He looked up at Susan and asked her to sit on the side of the bed. She sat down and put his hand in her hands.

"You see the little angel?"

Susan looked across the bed to the nightstand.

"This little angel has been more inspiration than you can imagine."

Susan looked at Jack and then back at the angel.

"Jack, I think she's beautiful. I love her simplicity. I especially love her little rusting wings."

Jack looked at the sparkling wings with a sense of frustration, knowing that Susan didn't see what he saw.

"Susan, she's more than that. She helps me look into my heart and soul. It's been years since I've done this, but when I do, I see her wings shine." Jack tried to sound convincing. "She doesn't move. She doesn't speak. She simply, well, inspires me, I guess."

Seeing a puzzled look on Susan's face, Jack said, almost in exasperation, "I can't explain it, I just know it's real."

Susan looked to the angel and back at Jack.

"And the envelopes?"

"I can't explain them either. All I know is that they were delivered in an envelope to intensive care with no return address. Monica dropped them off just after ten last night. I'm supposed to open one envelope each day for twelve days. Today was the first day. I set my alarm for midnight last night because I couldn't wait to open the first envelope. And this card is what I found."

Susan looked at Jack, at the angel, and then back at Jack.

With a kind smile, she said, "Do you think it's your medication?"

"Sometimes I wish that were so," Jack replied. "No, Susan, this is real." That word again.

Susan glanced at the angel's rusty wings, then stood up.

"Jack," she said, "I believe you. It's clear to me that something unusual has come over you. And it's a good thing. No, it's a wonderful thing; I'm just not sure I understand."

Jack looked at the angel.

Patience.

Jack turned back to Susan.

"It's all right if you don't understand. I'm not sure I do, either. I do know it's not for me to explain."

Susan smiled, leaned over to give Jack a kiss, and said, "I love you."

Jack looked at the angel, at the yellow carnation, at the donuts on the red plate, and then into Susan's eyes.

"I love you, too. And I absolutely know that God is in control."

Susan gathered up her things to leave.

"I'll be back in a little while. We're off to church. After that, I thought I'd treat Mom and Dad to a nice brunch."

Jack murmured, "Great. I wish I could go along."

"You will soon."

Jack looked to the angel once again.

Patience.

As she was departing, Susan looked at the angel. This would be the last time she saw rust on the wings.

Susan sat in church with her parents and her children. She could not stop thinking about Jack and the angel. It had been one long week, almost to the moment, since that police sergeant had told her the awful news.

Susan had watched Jack stabilize and then begin the long struggle toward recovery this past week. But she'd also seen something else: a deeper and unexpected spiritual renewal. Jack seemed to be changing right in front of her eyes. He'd always been smart about promoting his career, but now Jack seemed eager to reinvent his whole way of life.

Susan wasn't quite sure what to make of all this. It seemed like Jack was certainly focused on some things that were also important for her. Her life had been busy. She'd always talked about the importance of self-development—workshops, health clubs, and sometimes even church. She'd felt good about her plan, but didn't pursue the opportunities to grow in her spiritual life and values.

What she now saw happening to Jack looked different. More than a train had hit him. Susan wasn't sure what was going on. Frustrated in her confusion, all Susan could think of was that card Jack got:

God is in control. Always.

And what was that angel all about?

Don't obsess over the details. Just accept these simple messages over the next twelve days.

Susan sat up straight. She felt calm and energized. There were no answers yet, but she felt less of a need to have them right now. She couldn't wait to see what the next eleven messages said.

Susan's mind stopped racing. For the first time since Jack's accident, she felt relaxed. Looking around the crowded church, Susan wondered how many people felt at peace, or took the time to live their lives from moment to moment.

By the time the family got to brunch, everyone but Chip was in great spirits. Today he was quiet. Susan asked if he was okay.

Chip forced a smile. "Just missing Dad."

Susan knew this had been a terrible week for Chip. He was so close to his dad, his hero.

Suddenly she had a moment of inspiration. Since the next day was Martin Luther King Day, a school holiday, she asked Chip if he'd like to spend the night with his dad. He could do his homework at the hospital. Chip perked up.

"Sounds great!"

A light snow had begun to fall, putting a nice new coating of sparkling white on the entire city.

Jack was just waking up from a nap when everyone arrived. He was not happy about having to put up with another session of physical therapy in the afternoon.

Susan was the last to walk in. She set her purse on the window ledge and walked over to kiss Jack. After answering a dozen of Jack's questions about church and the brunch, Susan asked him if he would like an overnight guest. As Jack scanned the room, Chip's broad smile made it clear who his guest would be. He was thrilled.

Everyone started chatting. No one noticed when Susan walked over to the nightstand, and no one noticed as she picked up the angel. She looked at Jack, who was talking with her parents, and then she looked back at the simple little angel. She had never really noticed the details.

Chip walked over to his mom. He smiled.

"I'm sure glad that Monica brought that angel to Dad. I remember when she let me give it to him. He couldn't see it, so I told him what the angel looked like. I guess I saw it better when I had to tell Dad."

Susan listened to Chip while she studied the angel: the unique curves, her outstretched arms, the anonymous face. And those white wings. Sparkling white. She felt grateful for the angel.

Then she heard Chip ask about the envelopes on the nightstand. Chip saw the first card opened and displayed on the crowded table. He picked it up and read the words,

God is in control.

He opened the card and saw:

Always.

"Where did these come from?"

"They're a gift," said Susan. "We're not exactly sure who sent them."

Susan set the angel down. By this time everyone in the room had noticed the stack of envelopes. Katie ran over.

"Can we each open one?"

"Eventually," Jack said. "But my instructions are to only open one a day."

Katie sat on the side of Jack's bed. "What's the game called?"

Jack laughed. "It's a gift, not a game."

Bobby joined in, asking where the cards came from.

After thinking it over, Jack said, "We're really not sure. We're just pleased they're here." Fortunately, no one asked any more questions. Jack didn't have the answers.

Everyone enjoyed the afternoon together. Chip was excited when the others went home and left him with his dad.

Susan had given Chip some money to get dinner and break-fast, and Chip had just returned with his takeout bag from the cafeteria as Jack's dinner tray was being delivered. Chip couldn't have been more pleased to be sharing this meal with his dad, just the two of them.

After dinner, Chip did some of his homework. When he finished, he sat on the side of Jack's bed. Chip wanted to talk. He picked up card number one. For the next hour, Chip and Jack talked about serious things like humility, trust, and faith. Chip's questions surprised Jack. They were sharp and surprisingly mature. Jack didn't always know what to say, but now and then he got a little help from the angel.

Eventually, Jack said he was ready to sleep. Chip excused himself, left the room, and came back five minutes later with a roll of tape. He taped the first card beneath the first of the twelve flower arrangements that sat on a long shelf along the wall.

In the morning, Chip got muffins from the cafeteria. After a relaxed breakfast, Jack picked up the second envelope. He handed it to Chip with a smile. Chip sat on the side of Jack's bed and opened the envelope. As he pulled the card out, he noticed the words were printed upside down. He flipped the card and read the cover:

Start living upside down.

They both laughed and Jack said, "I suppose it wasn't a printing error."

Chip opened the card to find these words:

Life is mostly a paradox. Learn to live below the surface.

Chip squinted. "What's this mean?"

Jack thought for a moment. "I'm not quite sure. I'll have to think about it."

Chip stood up and went around the bed to get another piece of tape. He walked towards the plant ledge and hung the second card under the second arrangement. He hung it right side up, which made it appear upside down.

A few moments later, a substitute physical therapist came to take Jack to his morning session. Jack had been enjoying Chip's visit so much that he'd forgotten he had work ahead of him. Chip gave his dad a hug on the way out the door and said he'd finish his homework while he waited for his return.

Jack took a glance at the "upside down" card on his way out the door.

Don't be puzzled. We'll think about this as you suffer through this next therapy session, hurting to get better.

Jack shrugged off the angel's comment and set off for his workout.

Everyone else was moving through the corridors so fast. Jack felt lucky to be moving at all. As he shuffled along, Jack kept thinking of the words "below the surface." Then he remembered the second card, hanging upside down in his room. The meaning became clear: We see life the way we choose to.

Though the angel was nowhere in sight, Jack got the message as if she were.

Jack, you broke the code of the second card faster than I thought you would. In this world, most people live on the surface. But the surface can be deceptive. So many people never choose to look, much less live, below the surface. Jack, you need to look beyond appearances. You need to find what's real.

The pain of physical therapy was real. Jack's whole body felt inflamed each time he finished a session. Though he was improving, Jack felt more infirm as he labored to reach what seemed impossible goals for his battered limbs. Yet he couldn't help recalling the angel's message. He did want to see beneath the surface of his life, no matter the pain.

As his physical therapy session ended, Jack was anxious to see Chip again. He hoped they would talk about living upside down. Maybe this was a lesson they could learn together.

As Jack returned to his room, ready to reveal the insight of the second card, Chip had just completed all his homework and was writing a list on a sheet of paper. Before Jack could speak, Chip jumped to his feet.

"Dad, I've been thinking a lot about today's card. I think it's about opposites—contradictions. I don't know for sure, but I think it's about seeing things as 'both' rather than 'either-or.'"

Jack thought about Chip's words. As he looked at the card hanging on the ledge, he focused on the word "paradox." He grinned at his son's insight.

"I think you're right."

He asked about Chip's list. Chip walked over to the bed, sat down, and showed it to Jack.

"Just for fun," said Chip, "I decided to start listing a few opposites. Didn't get too far, but I did get a few."

Jack looked at Chip's list of opposites and other reflections:

Less is more.

In giving, we receive.

You can't keep love . . . because love isn't love until you give it away.

The last will be first.

We find strength in weakness.

In our sorrow, we find joy.

The consumer is consumed.

Sometimes you have to let go to hold on.

Silence can speak volumes.

We often make assumptions on the surface, and from these assumptions we make decisions and take action. It just seems like the productive and efficient thing to do. A world of speed rewards distance, not depth. But life is not a road to be paved on the way to a destination. It is a diamond to be experienced from many angles. It's not about where you arrive, it's about who you become.

Susan's parents had decided it was finally safe to head home. They made a quick visit to say good-bye to Jack and pick up Chip. Jack thanked them profusely for all of their help.

Jack was dreading the next day. With parental departures, school, and Susan needing to catch up on a few chores, it would be the first day Jack would be by himself. Physically, it wasn't a problem. Emotionally, it was a different story.

However, exhausted from another long day, Jack still slept through the night. He woke at dawn to hear the angel.

You're amazing me with your patience. But why are you feeling so lonely today? Did you forget about me?

That caught Jack by surprise. In fact, lost in reverie, he hadn't thought of the angel for a while.

I'm pleased with how much you've been thinking about our first two messages.

"Thinking about them and acting on them are two different issues."

I understand. I'm far more concerned with those who act before they think.

That comment prompted Jack to recall the fast pace he'd gotten used to at the office. He knew people were forced to act fast on the job, before they'd had a chance to think about their actions. He'd done the same sometimes.

Suddenly Jack felt a little sad. Except for the flowers from the office, he hadn't heard a word from his boss since the accident. Maybe that was just the way it was when results were the only thing that mattered.

So are you ready to open the third card?

"Ready."

Jack reached for the yellow envelope marked with a number three. His hands were still a bit shaky, but he managed to work the card out of the envelope. The card showed a beautiful white home surrounded on three sides by a generous porch.

"This is beautiful. Is it supposed to be my dream home?"

Hardly. Open the card.

As he opened the card, Jack read the third message:

There's no front porch.

Unless, of course, you build one.

As a child, he'd always dreamed of owning a home with a large front porch. That was a cherished vision of his future. He'd imagined a beautiful swing to the right side of the front door. The porch would be wide and long. Beautiful and peaceful. It would be a place to rest and think. Jack never found that porch as a child, and gave up looking for it as a man.

When Jack looked at the angel, he knew this card was not about a place. It was about time; the way he spent his time. The card was all about priorities. And it was related to the first two cards that he'd received.

Jack looked out the window. The snow was just beginning to melt. Bushes and flower beds were revealed beneath the white shroud as the snow cover shrank.

Jack thought about the Sabbath. The sacred lay concealed beneath the hustle of making a living. Though commerce might ignore the Sabbath, that did not change its nature or the human need for it. Jack decided at that moment to create a Sabbath in his own life. And he wouldn't blame others for his lack of focus and bad habits.

Jack, you're wise not to blame others for what's missing in your life. Taking ownership of your life is essential. That's when you start to find the real value in life. But it's not about pleasure. It's about a life lived with purpose. Despite all the choices and distractions that tempt you, remember that less is more. Your new front porch may help you discover what you need to ignore.

Jack was beginning to see how his daily messages were interdependent. He decided to build his "front porch." It might be small to start, but he would use it all the time.

He pulled out the pad of paper that Chip had left by his bed. He labeled three sheets: one "Daily," one "Weekly," and one "Monthly." Then he began to brainstorm all the things he could do on a regular basis that would help create his own version of a sacred place. He was determined to succeed.

After lunch, Jack reported for another session of physical therapy. Shortly after returning to his room, Dr. Berry popped in. Jack had begun to heal, and the doctor seemed amazed at his progress. Jack asked how soon he could go home.

Dr. Berry laughed. "Not so fast. One step at a time."

But Jack recalled the angel's promise, and was sure he'd stay just nine more days. Still arguing with the doctor in his head, Jack slipped into an afternoon nap.

Chapter 36

After a series of troubled dreams, Jack awoke without warning to a high fever. He felt awful. The medication didn't seem to help, and the nurses and doctor on call could not find the cause. Jack asked them to call Susan without alarming her. He knew that her parents had just left. The last thing she needed was unnecessary stress. He just wanted the staff to alert her.

By five o'clock in the afternoon, his temperature began to drop slightly, but he was nauseated and his bed was soaked with sweat. He couldn't even think about eating when his dinner arrived. He asked the nurse to take it away before she could place it on his food tray.

By eight that evening, his temperature had spiked to just under 105 degrees again. There was still no explanation.

Susan showed up an hour later with her overnight bag. She had spread the kids among their neighbors. Her lips were pursed with concern. Jack was disoriented and confused, and he looked over to his angel for a sign of hope. Her wings were as bright white as ever.

At eleven that night, Jack saw Monica come in. Her white uniform was the first thing he saw. Still confused, he thought his angel had come to life. He was about to thank Monica for coming to visit when she told him he was back on her floor, inside intensive care.

Jack still had no idea what had happened. But he heard the doctor talking with Monica and Susan, suggesting an alternative medication. Monica could see the disappointment in Jack's eyes—a setback like this when he'd been doing so well.

But Jack began to feel a little better by the middle of the night. By two o'clock, his temperature hovered around 102 degrees. He wasn't comfortable, but he did feel better. By sunrise, his temperature had fallen to 101. When Monica finished her shift, she came to Jack's room to sit with Susan and offer what comfort she could.

Shortly after midmorning, Jack's temperature dipped to just below 100 degrees. Though the doctor thought it best for Jack to remain in intensive care for the rest of the day, Jack wanted to return to his room. Monica agreed to keep an eye on his condition for several hours, and the doctor permitted Jack to return to the eleventh floor.

He arrived shortly before lunch and was hungry. Although he felt much better, Jack's confidence in his recovery was seriously shaken. He looked over to his angel, who had kept watch over his room during his stay in intensive care.

I didn't promise there wouldn't be setbacks. It's all part of your recovery. I did promise you'd go home on the twelfth day. Today is Day Four. Why don't you open your next envelope?

Susan sensed the angel's message. She asked Jack if she could open the fourth card. Jack nodded and watched her open it, just as Monica was walking in the room.

Susan ripped into the envelope and pulled out the card. She read the words on the cover out loud:

Life can be more difficult . . .

She opened to the inside verse and paused.

"What's it say?" Jack demanded.

Susan repeated the words on the front panel and continued with the inside verse:

when you have too much to lose.

It didn't take Jack long to figure out this one.

Monica offered her opinion as well. All three of them tossed around examples of the seductive power of possessions. They agreed that most people acted as though they believed more is always better.

Monica had seen such a struggle when her brother had lost his job while living in an expensive home. "The way to the top," she said, "can take awhile . . . but the fall can be sudden."

And the fear of falling can destroy you.

Jack recalled colleagues who were dynamic and outspoken when they began to climb the ladder of success. But the higher they climbed, the fewer risks they took. Often, they burned out at the top.

Jack had seen clients consumed by the value of their stock options. And CEOs who couldn't get enough. They all faced enormous pressure to keep the party going. But they all had an awful lot to lose.

After he finished mentally bashing the upper echelon of corporate America, reality set in. This card was in Jack's room for a reason. It wasn't for some top executive in a far-away place.

I wondered when you'd wake up. I thought your fever had affected your brain.

Jack was still feeling a bit weak, but he tried to keep up. "It's about addiction and entitlement. It's the difference between protective and proactive."

It's when the bottom line becomes the mission rather than the means. That's when your mission suffocates your passion. It's when you begin to die. Success is not a balance sheet and failure is not reserved for the worthless. How you view the meaning of success and how you see the value in failure most often determine what you're willing to lose. Remember that these daily messages are interdependent. You must be willing to lose if you ever really want to win. Just be sure that you never gloat about your victory. If you do, you'll need to go back to the first, and most important message: God is in control. Always.

The room was silent. All three of them were staring at the angel. Jack and Susan looked at each other and then at Monica. Monica smiled. The wings were brightly shining for all three of them.

Susan left in time to be home when the kids arrived from school. Monica departed shortly after. Jack was exhausted from his fever and the new medication made him sleepy. He dozed through much of the rest of the afternoon. He woke briefly to eat half his dinner, and went back to sleep, which may have been why he was wide awake, staring at the ceiling at one o'clock in the morning.

It was Thursday. A heavy snow was falling outside. Eight inches were on the way. It was no big deal after the blizzard a few days earlier. From his darkened room, Jack watched the snow float past his window. It looked cold outside, but he felt warm and cozy. His fever hovered just above 99 degrees.

Jack thought over the many questions that had passed through his mind during his first week in the hospital. Then he thought of each of the first four lessons he had learned in this second week.

God is in control. Always.

**Start living upside down. Life is mostly a paradox.
Learn to live below the surface.**

There's no front porch. Unless, of course, you build one.

Life can be more difficult . . . when you have too much to lose.

Lost in thought for more than two hours, Jack eventually noticed how quiet the eleventh floor had gotten. It was after three in the morning. The heavy snow still fell gently.

He looked away from the window toward the angel. Her wings reflected the whiteness of the snow.

Welcome to a new day, Day Five.

It hadn't yet dawned on Jack that it was a new day and that the fifth envelope was waiting for him.

I can see your patience or forgetfulness is working well this morning!

He ignored his angel's humor and reached for the fifth envelope. It was a bit thicker than normal. He pulled out the card. On the cover it said:

Know and value . . .

He quickly opened the card and found the rest:

your values.

Jack thought that was just common sense.

These are all common sense. Remember, Jack, don't be fooled by their simplicity.

Jack smiled and noticed that a small tablet had fallen out of the card. It was made of a fine-quality ivory paper. A soft watermarked note across the bottom read: "Instead of thinking about your values, write them down."

It had been some time since Jack had intentionally thought about what he took to be his core values. He was quite good at setting goals and executing to-do lists. But he'd never written down his values.

Always up for a challenge, he reached for the pen on his nightstand and figured he might write until sunrise. It was 3:21 a.m.

By 3:34, his pen had stopped. Jack was stumped. He couldn't find the words. He could only assume there must be more.

I see you're struggling.

"No, just temporarily stumped."

You're not alone. What seems most simple in concept is often most difficult in execution.

"I can tell. Guess I'm a little rusty."

You and pretty much everyone else who has to deal with today's fast-changing world.

Jack felt sad. He'd always thought of himself as a winner. He worked hard to win and was willing to do whatever it took.

Jack, don't be sad or disappointed. It's not about looking back. You need to focus on the present. That's the only place you can be-

gin. The past can teach you lessons, but offers little further value. And you can certainly build on what you've done. You've worked so hard to achieve what is seen on the surface and beyond. You've done little, however, to preserve your inner values. You're driven by your wants and needs. That's fine, as long as you nurture your core values.

Jack looked at the angel. "Let me think about that."

No, write down any and all of your thoughts.

Jack didn't like to journal or keep a diary of any kind.

I know you're not into journaling. Too much of a girl thing, right?

"Maybe."

Well, forget that. Not many women take the time to write down anything, either. Besides, you seem pretty good at writing down business plans, procedures, and to-do's.

"But that's different."

No, it's not. It's the same. When you write things down you get specific. You can see what you're thinking. You need to see the foundation of who you are, your depth. Why not give it your best effort?

Jack wasn't convinced. But reluctantly he started to write as the snow continued to fall. Within minutes, the pen was moving so fast it hurt his hand to keep writing. His mind was racing faster than his hand could possibly move. He wasn't sure if everything he wrote was really a core value, but he would dissect and prioritize later. Finally, exhausted from his writing binge, Jack fell asleep with the pen in his hand.

By morning, with the heavy snow clouds hanging in the sky, there was no winter sun to be seen. He woke at seven, thinking about his values and knowing he'd have a lot to talk with Susan about whenever she arrived. Jack guessed she wouldn't show up for another couple hours. He could write some more by then. The path to recovery seemed to coincide with the scribblings of a pen.

On an impulse, Jack reached for the phone and called Susan. He got the voice mail. Susan was probably running around getting the kids off to school.

He left a short message: "Susan, when you come to the hospital, please bring a pen and a tablet of paper. I love you."

Frazzled from getting everyone up and out the door, Susan took a quick shower, got dressed, and was about to fly out the door when she noticed the red message light flashing on the phone. She listened to Jack's message, but didn't think much about the request. She reached into the drawer under the phone and pulled out one of the many tablets Jack had brought home from a convention. She looked to see if she had a pen in her purse and then she was on her way to the bank, post office, and finally, St. Edward's Hospital.

Some time later, she burst into Jack's room, still breathless from her errands. Jack handed her the card of the day. She glanced at the cover:

Know and value . . .

Then she opened the card to read:

your values.

"Nice," was all she said.

Jack picked up his once-blank tablet and handed it to Susan.

"This is important," he said.

Susan flipped through all the scrawled pages of random thoughts. Jack sat quietly as she browsed some of the pages. Finally, she looked up at Jack and asked, "When did you do this?"

Jack responded, "While you were sleeping."

Susan looked back. "How long did it take you?"

"A couple hours." Jack knew what she was thinking. He needed his sleep. He quickly admitted, "I'm a little tired now."

Susan pulled a tablet from the bag hanging on her shoulder.

"I got your message. I can see why you needed more paper."

Jack grinned. "That tablet's not for me. It's for you! I thought if this exercise was good for me it would be good for you, and, ultimately, good for us."

Susan looked at the angel.

Yes, that tablet's for you.

Susan handed Jack's pages back to him. She didn't think this would be difficult because she had a regular habit of writing in her journal.

But you most often write about things, activities, and some-times your feelings. Rarely, if ever, do you dig into your values.

Susan decided to tape the fifth card in place, underneath the fifth flower arrangement.

As she was hanging the card, Jack's physical therapist walked into the room. Sheila stood taller than Jack. She was strong and decisive, too. But Jack had discovered a warmth and compassion lurking behind her stern expression.

Sheila noticed the string of cards taped under the flower arrangements. She walked around Susan to the first card on the left. She smiled as she read,

<hr>

God is in control. Always.

<hr>

She went down the line, reading each card in turn.

Then Sheila turned to Jack. "I love these cards. I've never seen this series before!" She went back to the first card. She seemed to want to talk about each of them. And Jack was glad to talk with her as long as she wanted. Anything to get out of physical therapy!

After a while, Sheila asked the obvious next question. "Are there any more?"

Jack pointed to the numbered yellow envelopes on his nightstand. "Yes," he said, "but just one a day."

Jack thought Sheila might ask where they came from. But no such luck. She reminded Jack that they were late for his physical therapy.

After they left, Susan sat down and started to write. It would prove harder than she had imagined. She wanted to grab Jack's tablet, but she kept writing. Before long, she'd written down some things that she hadn't thought about for years. She was still writing when Jack got back from therapy two hours later. They were both tired, but for different reasons.

Susan wanted to talk about what they'd written, but encouraged Jack to take a nap instead. Within minutes, he was sound asleep. Susan recalled that Chip had gotten his nights and days mixed up when he was a baby. Now her husband seemed to have the same problem.

By the time Jack woke from his nap, Susan had gone out and returned with one of his favorite junk-food lunches. No harm in that, she thought, as Jack enthusiastically gobbled it down.

After lunch, Jack was feeling great, ready to talk about their notes. They enjoyed switching tablets and reading the random thoughts each had written. For an hour or so they talked themselves hoarse.

They challenged each other's thoughts in a constructive way. Every now and then they'd each look at the angel. The angel did not respond, except once, to help them understand the real need of the fifth message on values.

Your values are your filters. They screen out behavior not consistent with your principles. If you don't maintain them, your screens develop little holes. Gradually, these holes expand until your values no longer filter out unhealthy behavior. You lose touch with what's at your core. But when your values work, they protect you. They limit and define your wants and needs. The fewer wants you chase, the more resources you have to get what you need.

Jack and Susan both agreed. This would not be a one-time exercise. It was demanding but enjoyable. It had been one of the best gifts they'd shared in quite a while. They'd opened themselves up to look inside.

Susan had to get home before the kids returned from school. She promised to come back with the kids if the snow stopped falling and if they didn't have too much homework.

Jack thought he'd take it easy for the rest of the day in case his family showed up after dinner. Because he couldn't seem to sleep, he grabbed the pages that he and Susan had written. He read them several times. Each time he discovered something new.

Then he took a new approach with his list. He began to wonder what made certain things on his list look more meaningful than others. With each phrase or thought, he began to ask why it was important.

His answer often revealed a new idea that wasn't yet on his list. Little by little, he began to arrange his ideas into groups of simple behaviors, wants, needs, and finally, real core values. There was no right or wrong, black or white, that defined the groups. They were just steps toward clarification in his mind.

Before he knew it, dinner had arrived. Though Jack wasn't too hungry after his big treat, he ate the entire meal. He wanted to get all the nourishment he could.

It was still snowing, but Susan knew the kids would be disappointed if they couldn't go to the hospital. When his family arrived, the kids ran to see the newest card hanging from Jack's shelf. Susan had kept it a surprise. As they talked about the idea of the day, Jack and Susan shared how they had written down what was important to them. Katie suggested that the kids could write something, too.

After about fifteen minutes, Chip decided to make a game out it. He suggested that everyone write down three things that they believed would or should be on each person's list. It didn't take them long. Everyone was surprised to find how much easier it was to write down ideas about others than it was to write values for themselves.

They went around the room clockwise, each person giving one idea at a time, and they were amazed at what they found. They were each reminded how often others could see things that they couldn't see within themselves. Sometimes they laughed at the honesty of the suggestions. Sometimes the suggestions were painful.

A couple of hours passed. When his family left, Jack thanked God for the gift of his family and the gift of that day.

The angel's first four messages had opened his eyes. The fifth message had reopened his soul.

Jack turned out the lights early to get a good night's rest, but he tossed and turned for a long time. Finally, he turned on the lights and pulled out his newly created list of values. He reviewed the list and thought back to the daily routine of his life before the accident. He recalled the many ways in which he'd failed to follow his values. He was surprised that he didn't feel remorse, but rather a renewed sense of hope for the future.

Mike called from Memphis a little before ten. After they talked about Jack's health for a bit, Jack told Mike about the cards. Mike wanted to know the details and was surprised that Jack had the discipline to open only one card each day. As Mike pressed Jack for more information, Jack couldn't help smiling as he thought of his angel's insistence on patience.

Jack decided to share the gift in the same way he'd received it, one card at a time. He said he'd give Mike the first message on the phone, and then ask Susan to send another message by e-mail each morning.

Mike tried one last time to at least get Jack to tell him the first five ideas, so they'd be "on the same page." But Jack wasn't budging. He'd give Mike the first, but not the rest.

They burst out laughing. The conversation was more appropriate for kids haggling over baseball cards than a couple of adults talking about life.

Mike said nothing after Jack gave him the first message: "God is in control. Always."

After an awkward silence, Jack said, "Mike, are you still there?"

After another pause, Mike responded, "I'm still here, and still trying to be in control."

Jack and Mike began to talk about the message, and what it meant to them. It was past midnight by the time they finished. Jack decided to tell Mike the second message, since they'd begun a new day.

Mike repeated it back to Jack. "Start living upside down. Life is mostly a paradox. Learn to live below the surface."

Jack knew this one wasn't as straightforward as the first. He told Mike to think about the second message and call him back over the weekend.

As soon as he hung up the phone, he reached for the sixth envelope. It was, of course, a new day for him, too. He ripped open the envelope and pulled out the card. On the front:

Redefine your dream.

This seemed logical to him. He knew he was going to have to change some things. He was going to have to change his focus. As he opened to the inside, Jack saw the message that would change his life:

Not of what you'll do . . . but of who you'll become.

He'd meant to open the card and then get some sleep, but he didn't want to turn out the lights. Instead, Jack lay in his bed looking up at the ceiling thinking of how much he had focused on the "what" in his life. He had always been focused on the what. He'd pursued excellence in all that he did. If he had ever thought of "who," it was only within the context of what. In Jack's life, what he wanted to do always determined who he would be. Now he knew he'd been living his life backward.

He thought about the second card.

Start living upside down. Life is mostly a paradox. Learn to live below the surface.

As he mentally turned his life upside down, Jack realized he had to concentrate on who he would like to become, not on what he wanted to do—just the opposite of the way he'd chosen to live his life up until now.

As Jack scanned the core values he'd written down earlier, he thought they looked like the right combination of principles to help him define who he would become.

He was just getting ready to turn out the lights when Monica opened the door to see if he was awake. Seeing all the lights still on, she walked into his room.

Monica noticed the new card lying on Jack's bed. She picked it up and read it. As she did so, Jack thought Monica knew exactly who she was and what her values were.

Looking up at Monica, Jack inquired, "Did you write this one? You seem to live this message. Nursing seems to be the way you've chosen to express who you are."

Monica touched his right arm. "You're too kind, Jack. I only wish it were so clear to me." She chuckled. "I work hard at keeping my focus on who I am, not merely on all the things I have to do."

She walked over to the sink and tore a piece of tape from the roll. She then taped the new card below the sixth flower arrangement. She began to read each card already taped on the shelf, pausing for a moment in front of each. Jack watched her and silently repeated the cards' messages. He'd memorized them all.

After reading the sixth card one last time, Monica turned to Jack. "That's a lot to think about. I wish more people would think of these things. I see so many people come through intensive care. They need to heal their bodies, but most miss the lessons to be learned through their suffering. And that means they miss the chance to grow. You're an exception." She smiled at Jack and left to return to her nursing duties.

Jack turned out the lights. He looked toward the angel in the dark and could still see the outline of white, sparkling wings.

Jack had just awoken when his breakfast tray appeared. He was in an unusual amount of pain. He had gotten used to the "good day, bad day" routine. Although he didn't like the pain, it didn't derail his focus or his hope for recovery. He wasn't, however, looking forward to his daily therapy.

Jack's floor was at capacity and to get a head start on a long day, Sheila came early for his physical therapy session. She walked in the room, said good morning, and immediately walked to the flower ledge to check out the latest addition.

She reviewed all the cards and then she and Jack were on their way. Sheila had grown quite fond of Jack and his determination, and Jack had been grateful for Sheila's steady guidance.

Jack was in a talkative mood. He asked Sheila lots of questions about her work and what she learned through those she coached. Making good use of Jack's therapy time, she kept him working through his session, but shared with him the insight she'd acquired in her work.

Sheila found her world to be a microcosm of life. She said, "So many people have to learn the most basic elements of life again when I'm working with them. They have to rediscover the things they took for granted. They also learn to appreciate the gifts they used to think of as entitlements." Jack knew firsthand about the focus and determination it took to make progress in physical therapy sessions. He knew exactly what Sheila was talking about.

But then she got him thinking. "Jack, I've always wondered why they call this physical therapy. Only a small part is really physical. It's mostly mental. Physical things must happen, but only in the context of mental focus. As much as people want to recover, most of them struggle with the mental investment it takes."

Jack paused. Upside-down living, he thought.

Without giving him the slightest break, Sheila looked at him and told him to get moving. Jack grinned, made a wisecrack, and started up again. He kept thinking about what Sheila had said.

As he looked around the room at the various patients taking first steps ever so slowly with sometimes-minimal results, he thought of the broken spirit at work. He thought of how we try to fix everything with physical measures. New plans, reorganizations, strategy retreats. He knew these were important physical things, but clearly not highest priority. Real recovery would only come through mental focus. He knew leadership in his company was always uncomfortable with the "soft" stuff. They were far more comfortable focusing on bottom-line initiatives. Jack now knew these two things were inseparable.

He continued to work through his session. He didn't enjoy his exercises, but he did enjoy talking with Sheila. Before he knew it, he was back in his room.

Jack took a nap. When he awoke, he still had about an hour before Susan and lunch would arrive. He looked at each of the hanging cards and then focused on the newest addition:

**Redefine your dream. Not of what you'll do . . .
but of who you'll become.**

He remembered that famous question from his childhood: what are you going to be when you grow up?" No one ever asked who he'd be when he grew up.

As an adult, the first question strangers asked him was, what do you do? He wondered why. Lost for answers, he finally looked at his angel.

I thought you'd never ask! Maybe it has to do with the need for visible success, and how you define it.

This made sense to Jack. He'd seen almost everyone in business defining success by the balance sheet.

Success is neither good nor bad. Success is neutral. How you define it leads you to goodness or deceit. If the what precedes the who, you'll likely connect to a misguided personal meaning of success. Most often, it'll be tied to position and money.

Don't misunderstand: there's nothing wrong with money or position. It's just a question of whether they are your means or your end. If they become your desired end, you have most likely developed a subtle, but powerful addiction. This is not intentional; addictions are not deliberately created. But intentional or not, the results are the same. Most addictions become increasingly hard to support.

In the case of addiction to material success, you create a lifestyle within a certain community. If going up is seen as success, I can guarantee you that going down is seen and felt as a painful failure. You begin to need what you want, rather than want what you need. And much like the greyhound at the dog track, you'll never catch the rabbit. That is, unless you are living intentionally.

Jack, no one's doomed forever. But it does take courage to change directions. Addictions are always painful to abandon. The cure itself is always a challenge, and often difficult. It takes a disciplined mind to give up anything. There's a tremendous resistance that you must break through to move forward.

Jack thought of a space shuttle. He thought of the energy and momentum that it took to launch this enormous machine. He then thought of the resistance it met as it tried to leave and then reenter Earth's atmosphere.

It takes a strong person to define success by who he or she wants to become. Jack reflected on the very few people he knew who had taken this road. He thought of Jeff, a partner at a large accounting firm who had walked away from enormous financial potential to become the director of ministries for a church. He thought of Dave, one of the most brilliant individuals he had ever met, who turned down lucrative offers from top law firms to join the navy in order to use his incredible mind to serve his country.

Work is only an arena where you can bring the who to life. Where you are is not near as significant as who you are.

Jack thought of Maryann, who had stayed the course of a financially rewarding career. But he knew she could easily leave tomorrow and find just as much joy and fulfillment in being a waitress. He couldn't help but think of the wonderful woman who usually worked the drive-through window at the nearby fast-food joint. Her spirit of service was so sincere. You couldn't resist her ability to lift your day through her cheerful attention. Both women pursued success tied to who, not what.

Susan arrived just as they were bringing in Jack's lunch tray. As he was served, Susan put her purse and a shopping bag on the chair and walked over to see the latest card. She read it twice and walked over to give Jack a kiss.

She had brought along a snack so they could have lunch together. For the first time since the Engaged Encounter retreat weekend they had taken just weeks before their wedding, they spent a whole meal discussing who they wanted to be. They were getting back to the basics.

After lunch, Susan opened the shopping bag. "I'm not sure you'll like this, but I think you need it." She pulled a journal from the bag.

Jack was surprised by his own reaction. He never thought he'd be excited about a journal. He'd rarely reflected on, much less written, anything personal.

Susan looked at Jack. "Life on the surface doesn't need a lot of documentation."

You have a point. Where there's little depth, there's little to discover.

As the winter sun began to rise on Saturday, Chicago was hit with another foot of snow. It had started much later than predicted, but fell much faster than anticipated. Following a very snowy December, it was shaping up to be a true Chicago winter with record-breaking snowfall. That didn't mean much to Jack, though, because he'd viewed much of the snow through the window of his hospital room.

He was glad the kids were able to come to see him after school on Friday afternoon, especially because it looked like they would be snowed in on Saturday.

After breakfast, he decided to open his next envelope. This was number seven:

You get what you measure.

He'd heard that a hundred times at work. The whole "quality" movement of the '90s had drilled that phrase into his head. He opened the card and read the rest of the message:

Make a plan.

The inside verse was what he was expecting. That was one of many disciplines the workplace had taught him. It just never occurred to him to take the same disciplines and use them elsewhere in his life. What took him by surprise was the small phrase at the bottom of the inside flap:

Use your journal.

After all that had happened, Jack wasn't sure why he was surprised by anything. He looked over at his nightstand and saw the journal that Susan had brought him the day before. He knew he would begin building a plan today. But that would have to wait until after physical therapy.

Since he had a few minutes to spare, Jack called Susan and the kids on his cell phone. Chip answered. Jack was delighted to hear that Chip wanted to come spend another night at the hospital. He hoped the road crews would help make it possible. He talked to Bobby and Katie, who each lifted his spirits to new levels. Finally, he spoke with Susan.

She immediately asked if he had opened the seventh card. Jack couldn't wait to tell her about the card—not so much about the verse as what followed it. He had a sense this card had a double message.

He shared the last sentence with Susan: "Use your journal."

Susan was silent on the other end of the phone for a moment. Jack interrupted the silence,

"Susan, are you still there?"

Finally, Susan responded. "Yes, Jack, but you won't believe me about that journal. It's been a busy week. And ever since you told me about these cards, I've had a strong feeling that I should buy you a journal to capture your thoughts. I kept resisting the idea—first because I was busy, and then because I didn't think you'd use it. But each day the feeling kept getting stronger. Finally, I couldn't resist it any longer. I was halfway to the hospital yesterday when I simply had to get you a journal. It seemed insignificant that it would take me twenty minutes out of my way."

Jack appreciated all that she'd done, including going the extra miles. Just as they were saying good-bye, Jack remembered he'd promised Mike an e-mail message each day as long as the cards lasted. He asked Susan to send his buddy the third message. Jack didn't know exactly what effect the messages had on Mike, but he hoped they might make a difference.

Sheila soon stormed in all ready for his next physical therapy session.

This session was the best yet. Jack was gaining strength and confidence in his ability to meet the physical demands of his therapy. In fact, he wasn't even tired when he returned to his room. Instead, he took out his new journal and began to write out a plan for his life. He just wasn't sure where to begin.

Don't make this complicated or overwhelming.

Jack realized how well the angel knew him! He was always making things more difficult than they needed to be.

Forget what you do. Go back to your list of core values. They're the foundation of all you'll become. Think through them and begin to write about who you want to become. Try to capture your thoughts in three or four sentences.

To get there, first write a lot of sentences. Check them all and see how you can merge and tweak them. Look through your words and see where you can find common themes. Eventually your three or four sentences will emerge.

Jack started drafting his sentences. After writing about fifty lines, he went to work on the fine-tuning. In the midst of his frustration, he looked again at the angel.

Don't look for perfection. There's no such thing. This is just a starting point. My friend, you're a work in progress. If you look for perfection, you'll never get started.

As he experienced the freedom of imperfection, some helpful ideas began to surface. He finally turned to a clean page of his new journal and wrote down five sentences. Jack looked pleased and thought, okay, so I'm one sentence over budget.

Close enough! And enough for today.

As Jack was closing the journal, a hospital dietician walked into his room. He'd seen her before, but didn't know her name. She set his lunch on the bed tray and pushed it into position over his bed.

"Anything else I can get you?"

Jack thought her question sounded almost automatic.

"No thanks," he replied. "It looks fine." But as she began to leave, Jack asked her name.

She turned around with a big smile. "Martha."

"Martha, I just wanted to let you know how much I appreciate your helpfulness." She had a beautiful smile.

Martha told Jack he was most welcome and left. Jack felt pleased to have brightened Martha's day in such a simple way. He was learning to slow down and express his gratitude for so many good things he'd always ignored on his way to big results.

But the day wasn't over. Right after lunch, someone unexpected walked through Jack's door.

Tim, the young train conductor, looked much better than he had during his first visit to the hospital.

Jack was glad to see him again, and let Tim know it. They were both relaxed in each other's company, although it had only been days since they met.

They talked about Jack's condition, and at the end of the conversation, Tim told Jack how glad he was to see his progress. Then he stood up to leave, so as not to wear out his welcome. Jack looked at the six cards hanging on the wall and thought of the seventh one sitting on top of his journal.

He asked Tim if he was in a hurry.

"No, I'm off until Monday."

"Tim, I'm doing much better, but my mental recovery is the best gift I've had," Jack told him.

The young man looked puzzled. Jack wasn't sure what to say next.

Don't look for perfection. There's no such thing.

So Jack told Tim about the cards. Jack was surprised when Tim asked for the napkins from the dinner tray so that he could copy the messages. They talked about the messages and their meanings over the next couple of hours.

Although the two men led entirely different lives, the train wreck that had brought them together seemed about to change them both for the better. This time spent with Jack opened up Tim's mind to a fresh look at life and his own potential.

As soon as Tim left, Jack called Susan. She told him the roads were clear enough and Chip would stay the night with him.

Jack told Susan about his visit with Tim, and asked her to pick up another journal. He wanted to send it to his new friend.

The falling temperatures had started refreezing some of the salted roads, making the drive very slow. Susan and the kids arrived around seven o'clock.

The family played a couple of games, then Susan got Bobby and Katie ready to go home. By ten o'clock, they were on their way.

Chip taped up the seventh card and unpacked his bag to get ready for bed. But then he and his dad began to talk about the cards again, about what they each would do to make the messages real in their lives. Jack couldn't exactly say he was thankful for his wreck, but he was deeply grateful for his angel and the chance he had been given to start again.

After a long discussion, father and son fell fast asleep. Neither moved until the door hitting the wall woke them up. It was time for breakfast.

Chip rubbed his eyes and stretched. He searched his overnight bag for the meal that his mom had made and joined his dad for breakfast. As soon as they finished, Jack handed the eighth envelope to Chip, who pulled out the card and read the front panel out loud:

Changing is easy.

Neither of them knew exactly what to think about such a simple promise. Father and son both knew how tough change could be. Then Chip opened up the card and read aloud the inside verse:

Sustaining change is hard.

Chip knew that for sure. Even at his age, he remembered how few New Year's resolutions he had actually kept.

Jack grimaced at the thought of "change initiatives" in the business world. Change had become a way of life at work. Yet, somehow, the changes never seemed to matter.

"The more we change, the more we stay the same." Jack thought this cliché described the lack of merit in most changes in life and the workplace. Change rarely measured up to expectations.

Maybe expectations were part of the problem. Jack knew most people lived in the past or the future, hoping to dodge the limits and demands of the present.

Then it hit him. He looked at Chip. Jack thought of the people he knew who had been through real change. Not a small adjustment that might have seemed big at the time, but real change. In every case that Jack could think of, he realized that the person affected had grown significantly.

He told Chip that constructive, real change made people stronger. It helped them become better, healthier human beings. They moved forward with greater confidence.

Jack talked about a few people he'd known who'd gone through great change in their lives. He told Chip never to fear a challenge, change, or tragedy. He now realized these could be straight paths to personal growth and fulfillment.

Susan picked up Chip after lunch. She couldn't stay long, since she had a list of chores to do before school resumed on Monday.

Before she left, Jack reminded her to send Mike his next e-mail. She told him she'd sent it earlier that morning. Jack wondered what Mike had thought of one of the most difficult cards:

Life can be more difficult . . . when you have too much to lose.

After they'd all gone, Jack took a nap that lasted all afternoon. When he awoke, he couldn't believe he'd slept so long. If it hadn't been for Martha bringing in his dinner tray, he might have slept through the night. Jack didn't know why he was so tired. It had been nice having a day off from his physical therapy.

After dinner, Jack began to write in his journal again. He wrote whatever came to mind. He'd have plenty of time later to edit and prioritize his thoughts.

As Jack looked across at each of the cards, he had a strong feeling that his endurance was getting better.

He looked over at the clock. It was after midnight. Jack felt pretty good about what he'd accomplished so far.

A wonderful beginning.

Somehow, a beginning seemed just fine to Jack. He was tired of mindlessly checking off entries on life's to-do list. He realized that the object wasn't to finish. He now knew most people never really even got started.

It was a new day, but he resisted the temptation to open the next envelope. He was mentally and physically drained. Jack wanted to check out the next card when he was fresh.

Your patience is amazing.

Jack smiled and was pleased to be making progress. He wondered if it would last in the world outside.

Chapter 44

By five o'clock Monday morning, Jack was wide awake. His spirits were high and he was eager to go home. He knew his physical therapy would continue after his departure, but all he could think about was his own home and his own bed.

He decided to beat Susan to the punch in getting the next message to Mike. He knew that Mike would be up and getting ready for work, so he called. Jack was right. The two men talked for quite a while because Mike was in no hurry.

As soon as Jack hung up the phone, he reached for the ninth card. It read:

Genuine relationships are God's greatest gift.

Jack paused. He couldn't help but think of the many people he'd been blessed to know. So many wonderful people. He looked inside the card.

Love is what matters.

There are many kinds of love, Jack thought. And he'd failed to love in so many ways. Love and busyness don't mix too well. As he thought about the pace of life in America, he began to wonder if anyone really remembered how to love.

Jack couldn't help thinking about how connected he was to so many people. He had a lot of networking contacts, but these contacts did not amount to a real community. He was pretty sure other people were in similar situations.

Jack knew he loved Susan and his children, although his actions did not always show it. But did he love others? Could he love others? Was he capable?

Sometimes. If you choose. And yes.

Jack whipped his head around to face the angel.

You forget about many whom you should love. You're so busy building a network that you're forgetting to love and cherish the relationships you already have. As you work to add more and more people to your network, you undermine your ability to enjoy the people you already know.

So many people suffer from a need to be interesting. Celebrities want to be interesting and everyone else follows their lead. Everyone is trying to outdo everyone else so as not to fall behind in the race for visible success.

Interest is the answer. But it's about being a person who is interested, rather than a person who is interesting.

Just after the terrorist attack on New York in 2001, Jack had seen love and kindness pour out across the land. Strangers united. Road rage faded. People reached across the nation to help one another and expected nothing in return.

But it simply wouldn't hold. It simply couldn't hold. Jack again wondered if everyone had forgotten how to love. Tearfully, he pondered if it would be possible for him to learn to love again.

Yes, if you're willing to sacrifice. You must be willing to lose if you want to learn to love.

Jack took out his journal and drew columns on a blank page. At the top of each column he wrote one of the roles he played in life: father, husband, professional, friend. Under each heading, he listed every person he knew who related to him through that role. He thought of names faster than he could write them. Was it possible to love this many in some way?

Sure. If it's a way of life.

He kept writing. One name triggered another. He didn't discriminate. He listed those he loved, liked, disliked, and even hated. Although he was tempted, he left no one off the list. Feeling good, Jack looked to his angel for praise.

That's a nice list of people you know. What about complete strangers?

"How would I list strangers?"

You can't, but love is not just for those you know. It's for all. It's a way of life.

Then the angel echoed the words read at Jack's own wedding.

Love is patient, love is kind. It's not jealous or pompous. It's not inflated or rude. It doesn't seek its own interests. It's not quick-tempered. It doesn't brood over injury. It doesn't rejoice over wrongdoing, but rejoices with the truth. It bears all things, believes all things, hopes all things, endures all things.

Jack felt deflated. He was so far away from living a life of love. He looked to the angel, almost with a sense of embarrassment.

Don't feel bad; you're ahead of most. At least you're listing people. Many others would be listing things. The concept of love has been greatly abused. You've probably heard: we love things and use people. We should love people and use things.

Jack felt a little better.
"I've been so busy, I guess I've been too busy to love."

It's not about "busy." There are many busy people who love. It's about motive. Busyness is only a problem when love requires you to stop and you can't.

"I suppose if I learn to love strangers as a way of life, then I'll naturally love the people on my list."

Not exactly. There are many who can love perfect strangers, but can't love the people they live with every day. It's more important to first understand the value of love and the joy it will bring to your life. If you develop a hunger to love, you'll soon find that there's no longer a need to differentiate friends from strang-

ers. Your motives will always be fed by love. Light defeats dark, and love defeats hate.

"I'm not sure I know how to do this, but I'm willing to do my best."

That's all you need. Know that likely you'll fail many times. But as you pick yourself up and try again, you'll move closer and closer to love.

Jack thought of all the workshops he had attended in his career: negotiating, customer service, team-building, handling tough clients, effective communications, and more. Jack thought it was strange that these workshops represented so many ideas and strategies for developing skills, but that no instructor had ever mentioned love.

He thought the best workshops could be presented in no more than fifteen minutes. He laughed as he imagined this scenario: "You want to give incredible customer service? Love them. You want to retain your employees? Love them. You want to build better relationships with tough people? Love them. You want to have effective teams? Love your teammates."

His door opened abruptly. It was time for breakfast. And soon enough, Sheila would come to get him for the next round of physical therapy.

He was ready to go to work on walking—and loving.

Chapter 45

Physical therapy was noticeably easier. It flew by, as did the rest of the day. Jack told Susan not to come to the hospital. She had enough to do. Jack decided that was part of love, too. He spent the afternoon with his journal.

After dinner he wrote letters to Susan, Chip, Bobby, and Katie. The letters were easy, so he also wrote to Susan's parents and his good friend Mike. He wrote from his heart, whatever seemed right. Each letter was therapeutic for a person learning to live a life based on love.

He was still writing when Monica stopped by at the start of her night shift. Jack showed her the ninth card. She taped it under the ninth flower arrangement, the only roses on the ledge. She could only stay a minute.

Right after Monica closed his door behind her, Jack said aloud, "There's someone who radiates love."

You're right, Jack. But you have the same potential.

It was time to sleep and Jack turned out the lights.

Mike called the next morning. He'd opened Susan's e-mail message earlier:

**Redefine your dream. Not of what you'll do . . .
but of who you'll become.**

He wanted to talk, and Jack was ready to listen. Mike talked a lot, and asked Jack many questions about the message. They stayed on the phone until Sheila showed up to take Jack for his daily workout.

Jack noticed that somewhere along the line he'd begun to look forward to the workouts. He was trying harder and paying more attention to his progress. The session that morning proved to be his best yet. Jack began to think more and more of going home.

Susan was waiting for him by the time he got back from his physical therapy session.

"So what's the message for today?" she asked playfully.

Jack realized he'd forgotten to open an envelope. He didn't usually forget such important things. He shrugged, picked up the tenth envelope, and handed it to Susan.

The cover read:

Freedom is not freedom . . .

And on the inside:

without responsibility.

Susan sat down on the side of Jack's bed.

If there's a gift that can truly be misused, it's the gift of freedom.

Jack and Susan looked at each other. They were thinking the same thing, but Jack spoke first. "Some people," he said, "love America more than God."

Jack and Susan loved their country. That's probably why they were concerned. Jack remembered being inspired by an idea that Viktor Frankl had proposed: namely, a Statue of Responsibility on the West Coast that would serve as a visible balance to the Statue of Liberty on the East Coast. Jack had been impressed by the idea ever since he'd heard of it. He knew that Viktor Frankl understood the issue, because he was a Jewish psychiatrist who had been imprisoned in a Nazi concentration camp during the Second World War.

Any blessing taken to an extreme and abused loses its value.

Susan walked over to the second card. She looked at the whole message:

Start living upside down. Life is mostly a paradox.
Learn to live below the surface.

"Complete freedom is no freedom at all," she said. Jack nodded agreement.

You're right. Total freedom becomes entitlement without responsibility, and an attitude of entitlement leads to destruction.

Susan thought about the country she loved. She wondered if it was too late for it to regain a sense of national purpose and passion. She and Jack shared a longing for a return to authentic corporate responsibility in America that was not dictated by government, but flowed from the hearts of leaders throughout business.

Jack reminded Susan that the card they'd just read was not about America. It was about them. Because, Jack explained, responsibility starts with the individual.

"We've got to change our own lives first. That's the key to changing business and America."

Susan knew that he was right.

After she taped up card number ten, Susan left to pick up the kids from school.

Jack continued to brood about freedom and responsibility. He had a feeling there was something more to this, like taking ownership.

It wasn't about perfection. The angel had made that clear. But it was important, Jack thought, to accept responsibility for failure and own up to the consequences. He wondered if Frankl's proposed Statue of Responsibility might get built somehow, with a little help from Jack and others who shared his views.

In the midst of these thoughts, Dr. Berry stopped in. He had some great news for Jack.

"Your recovery has been remarkable," the doctor said, "and if you continue to progress, I think we'll let you go home on Thursday afternoon."

Jack looked at his angel. This was no real news to him, but it served as a confirmation of the angel's prediction. He told the doctor he could hardly wait and was sure he'd be ready. But it wasn't just the thrill of going home that kept Jack grinning at the doctor. He was all set to start a new life.

Chapter 46

After dinner, Jack talked with Susan and each of the kids on the phone. He heard Katie screaming with glee when she learned that he'd be coming home on Thursday.

After his call, Jack wrote some more in his journal. By now, writing had become a habit. Elated by the prospect of going home, he couldn't sleep. Still restless and wide awake at midnight, Jack reached for the eleventh envelope. He savored the opening of this next-to-last card. The first part of its message was a promise:

True joy is found in the most unusual places.

He paused longer than usual before peeking at the second phrase inside the card. He knew that joy was different from happiness.

Yes, Jack, happiness is something you work toward. It can be elusive. Once you find it, sometimes it's either not what you expected or it disappears. Happiness feels good. It's a weak emotion, fleeting at best. Joy, on the other hand, is a state of mind that's always available. But you must be alert to feel it.

Jack was beginning to understand. He was waking up and had no desire to snooze ever again.

He opened the card and there it was. The simplicity of its message surprised him:

It's wrapped in stewardship.

Stewardship. Jack started reflecting. He thought about the joy of being a part of something bigger than yourself. He thought of the value in leaving something behind better than you'd found it. It was one of the corporate values that he'd heard so much about, but had so seldom seen in action. Jack thought stewardship was the opposite of the corporate behaviors that were frequently rewarded.

Jack meant to change that through his own example.

Jack woke up early again on Wednesday. He was all worked up about going home. Even so, he begged Susan not to come to the hospital until Thursday. She had a lot to do before he returned home.

The day flew by. Sheila was amazed at his recent progress. She would've been even more amazed had she known about the revolution in Jack's attitude and the insights he developed during his stay at the hospital.

He wrote thank-you notes on Wednesday afternoon. Then he called Mike, who wanted to talk about his own new plans after reading several of Susan's e-mails. They agreed to stay in touch from then on.

After dinner, Jack wrote a few more notes in anticipation of the big day. Though it was already late, Jack decided to review all of his cards except the twelfth, which remained unopened.

He was just looking at the first card when Monica stuck her head in the door.

"Are you still awake? I hear you're going home tomorrow!" She glanced at the angel.

"I'm so glad you're awake," she continued. "I've gotta run out at the end of my shift in the morning. I just wanted to say good-bye."

Jack couldn't help it; his eyes began to fill with tears. It surprised him because he seldom cried about anything.

Monica clasped his hand. Jack blinked hard and asked, "Do you have a minute?"

"Sure."

"Just as you walked in, I was about to review each one of these cards." He hesitated. "I was wondering if you'd like to read each one of them with me."

Monica smiled and walked over to the ledge where all the cards were displayed. She slowly began to read the first one aloud:

God is in control. Always.

She paused before moving to the second card. "Shall I pack them as we go?"

"Great idea."

Monica detached the first card from the shelf and gently pulled the tape off of it. Then she continued reading and removing each of the remaining cards …

**Start living upside down. Life is mostly a paradox.
Learn to live below the surface.**

There's no front porch. Unless, of course, you build one.

Life can be more difficult . . . when you have too much to lose.

Know and value . . . your values.

**Redefine your dream. Not of what you will do . . .
but of who you will become.**

You get what you measure. Make a plan.

Changing is easy. Sustaining change is hard.

**Genuine relationships are God's greatest gift.
Love is what matters.**

Freedom isn't freedom . . . without responsibility.

Monica walked over to the bed and picked up the eleventh card. She looked at it a moment, then read it to Jack:

**True joy is found in the most unusual places.
It's wrapped in stewardship.**

She smiled at Jack. "We've learned a lot over the last few days."

"Thank you, Monica. I've had so much to learn."

"We all need to learn," she said. "We're never done."

Monica looked at a box she'd been holding since she walked in. "Jack, I suppose you recall the extra angel I ordered when we thought yours might be missing?"

Jack nodded.

"Well, at first I thought I'd give it to someone else when you found yours. But I have decided to give it to you with the hope that you would pass her on to someone."

Monica put the box on his nightstand, gave him a hug, smiled, and departed.

Jack slept through the night until Martha woke him with the clatter of the breakfast cart the next morning. She was smiling and cheerful as she entered his room.

"Good morning, Jack. I hear you're going home today."

Still groggy, Jack managed a grin.

She arranged his breakfast on his tray and started to walk out, saying over her shoulder, "I'll be right back."

She returned with a tiny white vase holding a single yellow carnation. Martha placed it on Jack's tray and smiled. "I hope you enjoy your breakfast."

Jack was tickled. "Thank you so much, Martha. And thank you for all of your service during my stay here."

Martha seemed to glow. "Thank you, Jack. You've made me grateful for my job. In my five years here, you're the first patient to call me by my name . . . and the first one ever to say 'thank you.' Of course I appreciate that, but what I appreciate most of all is that you've helped me find the joy in being of service."

As Martha reentered the corridor, she was surprised to see two well-dressed men walking briskly toward Jack's room. Jack, too, was taken aback when his boss and the company's CEO stepped into his room.

Jack knew his boss had called the day after Jack's accident. Of course, at the time Jack couldn't take any calls. Three days later, the human resources department had sent flowers and a note offering sympathy and best wishes for a swift recovery. But their visit on his last day of hospitalization struck Jack as more than a little bizarre. He could almost understand a last-minute appearance by his boss—but what was the CEO doing there?

Neither man smiled. They got right to the point. His boss, Wilson, spoke a bit awkwardly.

"Jack, I called the day after your accident. They told me you couldn't take the call. Your accident upset the whole office. Everyone took it hard. I know HR sent you the official company response, but we're here today for a different reason." Wilson nodded toward Pete, the CEO.

Pete walked over to Jack's bed and shook his hand. "Jack, we're delighted to see you on the mend."

Jack smiled politely. He'd met Pete once before, when Jack's team had won a large new account for the firm. Since then, it was rumored around the office that Jack was a guy with a future—at least until the accident.

Pete looked around the room. "Your accident focused our attention on a big issue at the firm: the balance between work responsibilities and family commitments. I have to admit it's not always been a fair balance. When I heard you were coming in to work on a Sunday when you had your accident, I felt terrible. Wilson here tells me you've made a habit of that in the last year or so."

Pete paused to gauge Jack's reaction. Jack just stared at him. He couldn't believe his ears. Everyone at work knew Pete expected top performers to live for the company, just as he did.

The corners of Pete's mouth turned up ever so slightly. "My main point is, we need to make some changes. We're convinced we need a better balance between work and the rest of life. And we think you're the man to help us create and enforce a new balanced policy for the whole firm. We know you won't be coming back full-time for a while, but this is just the sort of challenge we hope you'll be up to while you're recovering."

Standing over Jack, Pete looked imposing. He was a tall man with a deep voice, and he was used to getting his way.

"Jack, will you help us get our values straight?"

Jack could hardly speak. He felt like crying, but swallowed hard instead. His voice thick, Jack simply said, "Pete, I'd be honored."

As Pete motioned for Wilson to step forward, Jack could see the glittering white of his angel's wings to the side of the two men.

That's it, he thought, and reached for the box that Monica had left the night before.

Holding out the box for Wilson, Jack said, "I'd like you to have this gift. It was given to me with the understanding that I'd give it to someone else."

Wilson took the box and thanked him, and Jack added in a confidential tone, "It's a long story that I'll tell you some day."

Jack looked at his angel on the nightstand and knew at once what else he had to do. It wasn't what he wanted. It was what he needed.

Before he could have second thoughts, Jack picked up his special angel.

"Pete," he said, "You have no idea how special this little angel is to me. She's been with me every day, every step of my recovery in body and soul. She, too, was a gift. And she was meant to stay with me for just a while. Now I'd like to give her to you in the hope that she brings you as much joy as she has brought to me."

Pete was taken by surprise. He took the angel and thanked Jack. "Whenever you're ready to return to work, we'll be glad to have you back."

"I look forward to it." Jack believed this meeting had given his job new meaning.

They all shook hands and then Wilson and Pete left the room, waving their angels in the air. Jack knew his angel would prosper in the executive suite. He wouldn't be alone in his new work assignment.

Pete sees only rusty wings, Jack thought, but that's okay for now.

Patience!

Chapter 49

Jack reached for the final yellow envelope. He opened it more slowly than he had any of the others:

Are you willing to start?

He knew the answer to that question: "Yes!"
Then he opened to the inside verse:

Alone.

Jack felt confused. Without thinking, he automatically looked over to his nightstand. It was empty. He was alone, and he closed his eyes in resignation.

But he heard the voice of his unseen angel protest:

Jack, you're not alone. You never will be. Remember your first and most important card? God is in control. Always.

Sure there'll be times when you may feel lonely. You see, very few people in the world really want to make the sacrifices necessary to bring about real change—the kind of change that makes the world a better place. But if you search, you'll find examples. And those examples will inspire you. This final message only asks if you are willing to start alone. It doesn't say that you will be alone. And now, we've got work to do.

I have one last thing to say. On your first day back at work, you'll receive a large envelope with two other sets of envelopes inside. Each will be numbered one through twelve. I think you'll know what to do with them.

Jack smiled and thought, "Remember, only one each day!"

Although his angel was gone, Jack felt the presence of God.

Jack actually enjoyed his final physical therapy session as an inpatient. Success was a wonderful thing. He thanked Sheila and asked her if she'd take the most beautiful plant from his flower ledge. She'd told him about her greenhouse during one of his sessions. He knew the plant would be in great hands.

Moments after Sheila left, Susan walked in, with the kids streaming behind. They carried helium balloons and a homemade sign: Daddy Come Home . . . or BUST! Susan had let the kids stay home from school for this special day. They'd been busy all morning with preparations for Jack's return.

Susan was more quiet than usual. She kept reliving that awful Sunday that now seemed so long ago. Yet in the last two weeks, she'd witnessed a miracle in her husband's life, and in her own.

Susan kissed Jack. "We've come to bring you home."

As they packed Jack's things, he told Susan what he'd done with the angels. Susan was pleased that Wilson and Pete had finally come to see him. She wasn't surprised at all that Jack had given them the angels. Jack was different now.

Dr. Berry popped in to say Jack was cleared to go home.

He could have walked out, but the hospital insisted on a wheelchair. The kids got a kick out of it. They tied the balloons to its handles and taped their sign behind the seat.

Each of the children grabbed something: Katie wanted to carry the roses. Bobby had the plastic bag filled with take-home hospital supplies. Chip had a small overnight bag. Susan noticed the damaged little box in which the original angel had arrived. She picked it up and asked Jack if he wanted it.

"Sure," he said.

They had everything—well, almost everything. Martha had agreed to distribute the rest of the flowers to other patients.

The kids tumbled out of the room, giggling and jostling each other. Susan and Jack were alone. "Are you ready to go?" she asked.

Without answering, Jack asked Susan for the angel's box.

When he found the gift-shop sticker on the box, Jack asked Susan to give him a credit card. Then he called the shop, got the owner on the line, and ordered a hundred angel figures. The owner said she could have them delivered in about a week.

Jack gave her the shipping address off a hospital notepad by the phone. He told her to send the angels to the attention of Monica in the ICU. When the shop owner asked about a card, Jack declined.

He told the owner, "She'll know who sent them."

Susan looked at Jack, and again asked, "Are you ready to go?"

He smiled at his children, who looked impatiently back at him from the hallway.

You'll never be alone.

"Yes, I'm ready to go."

About the Author

As a professional speaker, author, and consultant, John Blumberg speaks with organizations that want to create leaders of substance and cultures of genuine service.

John started his career as a CPA, but shifted his focus from numbers to people and spent fourteen years in human resources, including worldwide recruiting responsibilities in professional services. It was there that he became a student of the real world. In 1996, John left behind a firm and position he loved to pursue his dream to join the world of professional speaking. He has connected with audiences ranging from corporate executives to university students in ten countries on three continents.

In a world of exponential change, challenge, and uncertainty, John became increasingly convinced that life is not always what it appears to be on the surface ... and that maybe normal isn't always real. In his first book, *Silent Alarm*, he shares a powerful story of hope and courage for busy professionals and for all people looking for what is real in the journey of life.

He lives in Naperville, Illinois, with his wife Cindy and their three children, Ryan, Kelly, and Julie.

John can be reached through his website at www.keynote concepts.com.

Lessons in the Silence
A free downloadable discussion guide

Your experience of *Silent Alarm* doesn't have to end here. In fact, we hope your journey has just begun! And we hope you will take advantage of John Blumberg's offer for a free download of a complete companion discussion guide. It is perfect for self-reflection, book clubs and small groups.

This discussion guide is designed to help you bring to life your experience of *Silent Alarm* in a very practical and actionable way. Here you will see numerous questions that allow you to reflect or discuss your various insights ... all encouraging you to adopt a refuse-to-snooze attitude!

We hope you will also visit John's blog at http://john blumberg.typepad.com. Here you will see John's frequent reflections all designed to inspire you to "stay-awake" in your personal and professional journey. John would also encourage you to share you own thoughts and reflections on his blog.

We hope you will also consider signing up for John's complimentary electronic newsletter, *The Front Porch*. It is distributed via email on the last Thursday of each month ... with the sole purpose of creating a place for you to step back, sit down and ponder the bigger picture of business and life! To sign-up for your free subscription, simply visit www.keynoteconcepts.com and click on "Front Porch Newsletters" in the left margin of the Home Page.

Is your silent alarm ringing? We hope you will take advantage of all of these free offers and find joy in your journey ahead!